NORTH AMERICAN BIRD
ID CHECKLIST

A journal for backyard bird enthusiasts

Published by Cool Springs Press, a Waynick Book Group Company

101 Forrest Crossing Boulevard, Suite 100

Franklin, Tennessee 37064

(615) 277–5555

www.coolspringspress.net

ISBN-13: 978-1-59186-460-8

First Printing 2009

Printed in the United States of America

10 9 8 7 6 5 4 3 2 1

Art Director: Marc Pewitt

PHOTOGRAPHY

On the cover: Northern Flicker by Brian E. Small

Scott Shupe: Eastern Screech Owl, Golden Eagle, Great Horned Owl, Indigo Bunting, Northern Flicker (48), Tricolored Heron, Wood Thrush

Brian E. Small: Baltimore Oriole, Barn Swallow, Belted Kingfisher, Black-billed Magpie, Blue-gray Gnatcatcher, Blue Jay, Brewer's Blackbird, Carolina Chickadee, Carolina Wren, Common Redpoll, Common Yellowthroat, Double-crested Cormorant, Eastern Bluebird, Eastern Phoebe, Goldfinch, Great Black-backed Gull, Horned Lark, Northern Cardinal, Northern Mockingbird, Pine Siskin, Red-Eyed Vireo, Red-winged Blackbird, Ruby-throated Hummingbird, Rufous Hummingbird, Tufted Titmouse, Yellow-billed Cuckoo

Jupiter Images: Bald Eagle, Common Merganser, Red-tailed Hawk, Ruffed Grouse

NORTH AMERICAN BIRD
ID CHECKLIST

A journal for backyard bird enthusiasts

SCOTT SHUPE

COOL
SPRINGS
PRESS

FRANKLIN, TENNESSEE

CONTENTS

INTRODUCTION

This book contains a checklist of all species of birds that are native to the North American Continent. The American Ornithologists' Union checklist has been followed for common and scientific names. Some common names will have the symbol (R) after the name which indicates that species to be rare. The symbol (I) indicates the species is a non-native introduced species that has become established in some areas of North America.

One of the great attractions of watching birds, in addition to being beautiful to look at, is that birds are also ubiquitous creatures that can be seen everywhere. Thus, bird watching is a hobby available to anyone, anywhere, and it is free! At least until you become seriously hooked and begin spending money on better binoculars, more and more bird books, and new cameras, lenses, etc!

Belted Kingfisher

The keeping of a life-list has always been a common practice among dedicated bird watchers, and for many, it adds an element of excitement and challenge to the act of watching birds. Enjoying the natural beauty of a bird is enhanced by the challenge of finding and adding to the life-list a new species. Some birders will keep separate lists for home verses an overall life-list, and a separate list for birds seen on vacations and travel. In addition, bird photographers may wish to keep a list of species photographed. This booklet is designed to meet all those needs.

For each species listed herein, there is also space to include additional information such as date observed, location, sex of the bird, and other activities such as breeding, nesting, or the presence of young. By carefully and accurately noting this type of information, birdwatchers can often contribute to the constantly growing body of knowledge about the science of ornithology (bird study).

Many bird species are migratory animals traveling thousands (or tens of thousands) of miles annually. The date of their arrival in different areas during these migrations is of great importance to amateur birders as well as professional scientists. Of equal importance is information pertaining to whether or not the species nests within a certain region of the country. A personal life-list is a tool for recording this important information.

To the amateur, making a heretofore unobserved "early sighting" or "new breeding record" can be a source of pride and accomplishment, as well as an opportunity to contribute scientific data. To the professional scientist, such information is another piece in the puzzle of scientific endeavor, and the attempt to better understand the natural environment upon which we all depend. In many ways, birds are a barometer of the earth's environment. The decline of a particular species (or group of species) can be an important warning that significant changes are occurring that could ultimately affect the quality of life for humans on planet earth. Similarly, the earlier arrival of annual migrants from the tropics each spring, or nesting activity observed farther and farther to the north each year, could be an indicator of worldwide climate change.

Cedar Waxwing

There is a well-worn phrase among birdwatchers: "Create a birder, and you have created a conservationist." For this writer, this axiom has been proven time and again to be true. It is hoped this book will in some small way help generate a greater appreciation and concern for conservation efforts.

There are those, I suppose, who are immune to the beauty of birds and for whom the wonder and mystery of their migratory lifestyles and elaborate songs holds no special significance. Their poverty can and should be alleviated! Through the simple act of introducing another to the magical ability birds possess for enriching human life, one can contribute mightily to building a better world for all.

The *Northern American Bird ID Checklist* is arranged according to certain groups of birds. Specifically, the order, family, genus, and species of each appears at the beginning of each group, with additional families or subfamilies appearing as they change.

ANSERIFORMES ———— ORDER
(W A T E R F O W L)

A N A T I D A E ———— FAMILY
D E N D R O C Y G N I N A E ———— SUBFAMILY
(T R E E   D U C K S)

Space has been provided for each bird listed where you can check off your sighting and make a couple of notes regarding the date, location, and any other important information.

MOTTLED DUCK ○
ANAS FULVIGULA ———— GENUS & SPECIES

DATE_____

LOCATION_____

NOTES_____

_____

In addition to these features, there is a gallery in the middle of the book featuring many of the inspiring birds from our continent. The corresponding page number appears in boldface next to the bird name in the index.

Happy birding!

ANSERIFORMES

(WATERFOWL)

ANATIDAE
DENDROCYGNINAE
(TREE DUCKS)

BLACK-BELLIED WHISTLING DUCK ○
DENDROCYGNA AUTUMNALIS

DATE_____

LOCATION_____

NOTES_____

_____

FULVOUS WHISTLING DUCK ○
DENDROCYGNA BICOLOR

DATE_____

LOCATION_____

NOTES_____

_____

ANSERINAE
(GEESE AND SWANS)

CANADA GOOSE ○
BRANTA CANADENSIS

DATE_____

LOCATION_____

NOTES_____

_____

CACKLING GOOSE ○
BRANTA HUTCHINSII

DATE_____

LOCATION_____

NOTES_____

_____

BRANT ○
BRANTA BERNICLA

DATE_____

LOCATION_____

NOTES_____

_____

BARNACLE GOOSE (R) ○
BRANTA LEUCOPSIS

DATE_____

LOCATION_____

NOTES_____

_____

GREATER WHITE-FRONTED GOOSE ○
ANSER ALBIFRONS

DATE_____

LOCATION_____

NOTES_____

_____

SNOW GOOSE ○
CHEN CAERULESCENS

DATE_____

LOCATION_____

NOTES_____

_____

ROSS'S GOOSE ○
CHEN ROSSII

DATE_____

LOCATION_____

NOTES_____

_____

EMPEROR GOOSE (R) ○
CHEN CANAGICA

DATE_____

LOCATION_____

NOTES_____

_____

MUTE SWAN (I) ○
CYGNUS OLOR

DATE_____

LOCATION_____

NOTES_____

_____

TUNDRA SWAN ○
CYGNUS COLUMBIANUS

DATE_____

LOCATION_____

NOTES_____

_____

TRUMPETER SWAN ○
CYGNUS BUCCINATOR

DATE_____

LOCATION_____

NOTES_____

_____

WHOOPER SWAN (R) ○
CYGNUS CYGNUS

DATE_____

LOCATION_____

NOTES_____

_____

A N A T I N A E
(D U C K S)

MALLARD ○
ANAS PLATYRHYNCHOS

DATE_____

LOCATION_____

NOTES_____

_____

BLACK DUCK ○
ANAS RUBRIPES

DATE_____

LOCATION_____

NOTES_____

_____

MOTTLED DUCK ○
ANAS FULVIGULA

DATE_____

LOCATION_____

NOTES_____

_____

NORTHERN PINTAIL ○
ANAS ACUTA

DATE_____

LOCATION_____

NOTES_____

_____

GADWALL ○
ANAS STREPERA

DATE_____

LOCATION_____

NOTES_____

_____

AMERICAN WIDGEON ○
ANAS AMERICANA

DATE_____

LOCATION_____

NOTES_____

_____

EURASIAN WIDGEON (R) ○
ANAS PENELOPE

DATE_____

LOCATION_____

NOTES_____

_____

GREEN-WINGED TEAL ○
ANAS CRECCA

DATE_____

LOCATION_____

NOTES_____

_____

BLUE-WINGED TEAL ○
ANAS DISCORS

DATE_____

LOCATION_____

NOTES_____

_____

CINNAMON TEAL ○
ANAS CYANOPTERA

DATE_____

LOCATION_____

NOTES_____

_____

GARGANEY (R) ○
ANAS QUERQUEDULA

DATE_____

LOCATION_____

NOTES_____

_____

NORTHERN SHOVELER ○
ANAS CLYPEATA

DATE_____

LOCATION_____

NOTES_____

_____

LESSER SCAUP ○
AYTHYA AFFINIS

DATE_____

LOCATION_____

NOTES_____

_____

GREATER SCAUP ○
AYTHYA MARILA

DATE_____

LOCATION_____

NOTES_____

_____

RING-NECKED DUCK ○
AYTHYA COLLARIS

DATE_____

LOCATION_____

NOTES_____

_____

TUFTED DUCK (R) ○
AYTHYA FULIGULA

DATE_____

LOCATION_____

NOTES_____

_____

CANVASBACK ○
AYTHYA VALISINERIA

DATE_____

LOCATION_____

NOTES_____

_____

REDHEAD ○
AYTHYA AMERICANA

DATE_____

LOCATION_____

NOTES_____

_____

COMMON POCHARD (R) ○
AYTHYA FERINA

DATE_____

LOCATION_____

NOTES_____

_____

LONG-TAILED DUCK (OLDSQUAW) ○
CLANGULA HYEMALIS

DATE_____

LOCATION_____

NOTES_____

_____

SURF SCOTER ○
MELANITTA PERSPICILLATA

DATE_____

LOCATION_____

NOTES_____

_____

WHITE-WINGED SCOTER ○
MELANITTA FUSCA

DATE_____

LOCATION_____

NOTES_____

_____

BLACK SCOTER ○
MELANITTA NIGRA

DATE_____

LOCATION_____

NOTES_____

_____

HARLEQUIN DUCK ○
HISTRIONICUS HISTRIONICUS

DATE_____

LOCATION_____

NOTES_____

_____

COMMON EIDER ○
SOMETERIA MOLLISSIMA

DATE_____

LOCATION_____

NOTES_____

_____

KING EIDER ○
SOMATERIA SPECTABILIS

DATE_____

LOCATION_____

NOTES_____

_____

SPECTACLED EIDER ○
SOMATERIA FISCHERI

DATE_____

LOCATION_____

NOTES_____

_____

STELLER'S EIDER ○
POLYSTICTA STELLERI

DATE_____

LOCATION_____

NOTES_____

_____

COMMON GOLDENEYE ○
BUCEPHALA CLANGULA

DATE_____

LOCATION_____

NOTES_____

_____

BARROW'S GOLDENEYE ○
BUCEPHALA ISLANDICA

DATE_____

LOCATION_____

NOTES_____

_____

BUFFLEHEAD ○
BUCEPHALA ALBEOLA

DATE_____

LOCATION_____

NOTES_____

_____

RUDDY DUCK ○
OXYURA JAMAICENSIS

DATE_____

LOCATION_____

NOTES_____

_____

MASKED DUCK (R) ○
NOMONYX DOMINICUS

DATE_____

LOCATION_____

NOTES_____

_____

COMMON MERGANSER ○
MERGUS MERGANSER

DATE_____

LOCATION_____

NOTES_____

_____

RED-BREASTED MERGANSER ○
MERGUS SERRATOR

DATE_____

LOCATION_____

NOTES_____

_____

HOODED MERGANSER ○
LOPHODYTES CUCULLATUS

DATE_____

LOCATION_____

NOTES_____

_____

SMEW (R) ○
MERGELLUS ALBELLUS

DATE_____

LOCATION_____

NOTES_____

_____

WOOD DUCK ○
AIX SPONSA

DATE_____

LOCATION_____

NOTES_____

_____

MUSCOVEY DUCK ○
CAIRINA MOSCHATA

DATE_____

LOCATION_____

NOTES_____

_____

PODICIPEDIFORMES
(GREBES)
PODICIPEDIDAE

PIED-BILLED GREBE ○
PODILYMBUS PODICEPS

DATE_____

LOCATION_____

NOTES_____

_____

LEAST GREBE ○
TACHYBAPTUS DOMINICUS

DATE_____

LOCATION_____

NOTES_____

_____

HORNED GREBE ○
PODICEPS AURITUS

DATE_____

LOCATION_____

NOTES_____

_____

EARED GREBE ○
PODICEPS NIGRICOLLIS

DATE_____

LOCATION_____

NOTES_____

_____

RED-NECKED GREBE ○
PODICEPS GRISEGENA

DATE_____

LOCATION_____

NOTES_____

_____

WESTERN GREBE ○
AECHMOPHORUS OCCIDENTALIS

DATE_____

LOCATION_____

NOTES_____

_____

CLARK'S GREBE ○
AECHMOPHORUS CLARKII

DATE_____

LOCATION_____

NOTES_____

_____

GRUIFORMES
(RAILS & CRANES)
RALLIDAE
(RAILS)

AMERICAN COOT ○
FULICA AMERICANA

DATE_____

LOCATION_____

NOTES_____

_____

COMMON MOORHEN ○
GALLINULA CHLOROPUS

DATE_____

LOCATION_____

NOTES_____

_____

PURPLE GALLINULE ○
PORHYRIO MARTINICA

DATE_____

LOCATION_____

NOTES_____

_____

CLAPPER RAIL ○
RALLUS LONGIROSTRIS

DATE_____

LOCATION_____

NOTES_____

_____

KING RAIL ○
RALLUS ELEGANS

DATE_____

LOCATION_____

NOTES_____

_____

VIRGINIA RAIL ○
RALLUS LIMICOLA

DATE_____

LOCATION_____

NOTES_____

_____

SORA ○
PORZANA CAROLINA

DATE_____

LOCATION_____

NOTES_____

_____

YELLOW RAIL ○
COTURNICOPS NOVEBORACENSIS

DATE_____

LOCATION_____

NOTES_____

_____

BLACK RAIL ○
LATERALLUS JAMIACENSIS

DATE_____

LOCATION_____

NOTES_____

_____

ARAMIDAE

LIMPKIN ○
ARAMUS GUARAUNA

DATE_____

LOCATION_____

NOTES_____

_____

GRUIDAE

SANDHILL CRANE ○
GRUS CANADENSIS

DATE_____

LOCATION_____

NOTES_____

_____

WHOOPING CRANE ○
GRUS AMERICANA

DATE_____

LOCATION_____

NOTES_____

_____

GAVIIFORMES
(LOONS)
GAVIIDAE

COMMON LOON ○
GAVIA IMMER

DATE_____

LOCATION_____

NOTES_____

_____

YELLOW-BILLED LOON ○
GAVIA ADAMSII

DATE_____

LOCATION_____

NOTES_____

_____

RED-THROATED LOON ○
GAVIA STELLATA

DATE_____

LOCATION_____

NOTES_____

_____

PACIFIC LOON ○
GAVIA PACIFICA

DATE_____

LOCATION_____

NOTES_____

_____

ARCTIC LOON ○
GAVIA ARCTICA

DATE_____

LOCATION_____

NOTES_____

PELICANIFORMES
PELECANIDAE
(PELICANS)

WHITE PELICAN ○
PELECANUS ERYTHRORHYNCHOS

DATE_____

LOCATION_____

NOTES_____

BROWN PELICAN ○
PELECANUS OCCIDENTALIS

DATE_____

LOCATION_____

NOTES_____

ANHINGIDAE
(ANHINGAS)

ANHINGA ○
ANHINGA ANHINGA

DATE_____

LOCATION_____

NOTES_____

PHALACROCORACIDAE
(CORMORANTS)

DOUBLE-CRESTED CORMORANT ○
PHALACROCORAX AURITUS

DATE_____

LOCATION_____

NOTES_____

GREAT CORMORANT ○
PHALACROCORAX CARBO

DATE_____

LOCATION_____

NOTES_____

BRANDT'S CORMORANT ○
PHALACROCORAX PENICILLATUS

DATE_____

LOCATION_____

NOTES_____

NEOTROPIC CORMORANT ○
PHALACROCORAX BRASILIANUS

DATE_____

LOCATION_____

NOTES_____

PELAGIC CORMORANT ○
PHALACROCORAX PELAGICUS

DATE_____

LOCATION_____

NOTES_____

RED-FACED CORMORANT ○
PHALACROCORAX URILE

DATE_____

LOCATION_____

NOTES_____

FREGATIDAE
(FRIGATE BIRDS)

MAGNIFICENT FRIGATEBIRD ○
FREGATA MAGNIFICENS

DATE_____

LOCATION_____

NOTES_____

_____

SULIDAE
(BOOBIES)

NORTHERN GANNETT ○
MORUS BASSANUS

DATE_____

LOCATION_____

NOTES_____

_____

MASKED BOOBY ○
SULA DACTYLATRA

DATE_____

LOCATION_____

NOTES_____

_____

BROWN BOOBY ○
SULA LEUCOGASTER

DATE_____

LOCATION_____

NOTES_____

_____

BLUE-FOOTED BOOBY (R) ○
SULA NEBOUXII

DATE_____

LOCATION_____

NOTES_____

_____

RED-FOOTED BOOBY (R) ○
SULA SULA

DATE_____

LOCATION_____

NOTES_____

_____

PHAETHONIDAE
(TROPICBIRDS)

WHITE-TAILED TROPICBIRD (R) ○
PHAETHON LEPTURUS

DATE_____

LOCATION_____

NOTES_____

_____

RED-BILLED TROPICBIRD (R) ○
PHAETHON AETHEREUS

DATE_____

LOCATION_____

NOTES_____

_____

CHARADRIIFORMES
ALCIDAE
(ALCIDS)

ATLANTIC PUFFIN ○
FRATERCULA ARCTICA

DATE_____

LOCATION_____

NOTES_____

_____

HORNED PUFFIN ○
FRATERCULA CORNICULATA

DATE_____

LOCATION_____

NOTES_____

_____

TUFTED PUFFIN ○
FRATERCULA CIRRHATTA

DATE_____

LOCATION_____

NOTES_____

_____

CRESTED AUKLET ○
CERORHINCA MONCERATA

DATE_____

LOCATION_____

NOTES_____

_____

COMMON MURRE ○
URIA AALGE

DATE_____

LOCATION_____

NOTES_____

_____

THICK-BILLED MURRE ○
URIA LOMVIA

DATE_____

LOCATION_____

NOTES_____

_____

RAZORBILL ○
ALCA TORDA

DATE_____

LOCATION_____

NOTES_____

_____

PIGEON GUILLEMOT ○
CEPPHUS COLUMBA

DATE_____

LOCATION_____

NOTES_____

_____

BLACK GUILLEMOT ○
CEPPHUS GRYLLE

DATE_____

LOCATION_____

NOTES_____

_____

CASSIN'S AUKLET ○
PTYCHORAMPHUS ALEUTICUS

DATE_____

LOCATION_____

NOTES_____

_____

ANCIENT AUKLET ○
SYNTHLIBORAMPHUS ANTIQUUS

DATE_____

LOCATION_____

NOTES_____

_____

MARBLED MURRELET ○
BRACHYRAMPHUS MARMORATUS

DATE_____

LOCATION_____

NOTES_____

_____

KITTLITZ'S MURRELET ○
BRACHYRAMPHUS BREVIROSTRIS

DATE_____

LOCATION_____

NOTES_____

_____

XANTUS'S MURRELET (R) ○
SYNTHLIBORAMPHUS HYPOLEUCUS

DATE_____

LOCATION_____

NOTES_____

_____

CRAVERI'S MURRELET (R) ○
SYNTHLIBORAMPHUS CRAVERI

DATE_____

LOCATION_____

NOTES_____

_____

DOVEKIE ○
ALLE ALLE

DATE_____

LOCATION_____

NOTES_____

_____

PARAKEET AUKLET ○
AETHIA PSITTACULA

DATE_____

LOCATION_____

NOTES_____

_____

LEAST AUKLET ○
AETHIA PUSILLA

DATE_____

LOCATION_____

NOTES_____

_____

CRESTED AUKLET ○
AETHIA CRISTATELLA

DATE_____

LOCATION_____

NOTES_____

_____

WHISKERED AUKLET (R) ○
AETHIA PYGMAEA

DATE_____

LOCATION_____

NOTES_____

_____

CHARADRIIDAE
VANELLINAE
(LAPWINGS)

NORTHERN LAPWING (R) ○
VANELLUS VANELLUS

DATE_____

LOCATION_____

NOTES_____

_____

CHARADRIINAE
(PLOVERS)

AMERICAN GOLDEN-PLOVER ○
PLUVIALIS DOMINICA

DATE_____

LOCATION_____

NOTES_____

_____

BLACK-BELLIED PLOVER ○
PLUVIALIS SQUATAROLA

DATE_____

LOCATION_____

NOTES_____

_____

PACIFIC GOLDEN-PLOVER ○
PLUVIALIS FULVA

DATE_____

LOCATION_____

NOTES_____

_____

KILLDEER ○
CHARADRIUS VOCIFERUS

DATE_____

LOCATION_____

NOTES_____

_____

EUROPEAN GOLDEN-PLOVER (R) ○
PLUVIALIS APRICARIA

DATE_____

LOCATION_____

NOTES_____

_____

EURASIAN DOTTEREL (R) ○
CHARADRIUS MORINELLUS

DATE_____

LOCATION_____

NOTES_____

_____

WILSON'S PLOVER ○
CHARADRIUS WILSONII

DATE_____

LOCATION_____

NOTES_____

_____

SEMIPALMATED PLOVER ○
CHARADRIUS SEMIPALMATUS

DATE_____

LOCATION_____

NOTES_____

_____

PIPING PLOVER ○
CHARADRIUS MELODUS

DATE_____

LOCATION_____

NOTES_____

_____

SNOWY PLOVER ○
CHARADRIUS ALEXANDRINUS

DATE_____

LOCATION_____

NOTES_____

_____

MOUNTAIN PLOVER ○
CHARADRIUS MONTANUS

DATE_____

LOCATION_____

NOTES_____

_____

COMMON RINGED PLOVER (R) ○
CHARADRIUS HIATICULA

DATE_____

LOCATION_____

NOTES_____

_____

HAEMATOPODIDAE
(OYSTERCATCHERS)

AMERICAN OYSTERCATCHER ○
HAEMATOPUS PALLIATUS

DATE_____

LOCATION_____

NOTES_____

_____

BLACK OYSTERCATCHER ○
HAEMATOPUS BACHMANI

DATE_____

LOCATION_____

NOTES_____

_____

RECURVIROSTRIDAE
(STILTS)

BLACK-NECKED STILT ○
HIMANTOPUS MEXICANUS

DATE_____

LOCATION_____

NOTES_____

_____

AMERICAN AVOCET ○
RECURVIROSTRA AMERICANA

DATE_____

LOCATION_____

NOTES_____

_____

SCOLOPACIDAE
(SANDPIPERS)

SEMIPALMATED SANDPIPER ○
CALIDRIS PUSILLA

DATE_____

LOCATION_____

NOTES_____

_____

WESTERN SANDPIPER ○
CALIDRIS MAURI

DATE_____

LOCATION_____

NOTES_____

_____

RED-NECKED STINT (R) ○
CALIDRIS RUFICOLLIS

DATE_____

LOCATION_____

NOTES_____

_____

PECTORAL SANDPIPER ○
CALIDRIS MELANOTOS

DATE_____

LOCATION_____

NOTES_____

_____

SHARP-TAILED SANDPIPER (R) ○
CALIDRIS ACUMINATA

DATE_____

LOCATION_____

NOTES_____

_____

WHITE-RUMPED SANDPIPER ○
CALIDRIS FUSCICOLLIS

DATE_____

LOCATION_____

NOTES_____

_____

SANDERLING ○
CALIDRIS ALBA

DATE_____

LOCATION_____

NOTES_____

_____

DUNLIN ○
CALIDRIS ALPINA

DATE_____

LOCATION_____

NOTES_____

_____

RED KNOT ○
CALIDRIS CANUTUS

DATE_____

LOCATION_____

NOTES_____

_____

LEAST SANDPIPER ○
CALIDRIS MINUTILLA

DATE_____

LOCATION_____

NOTES_____

_____

BAIRD'S SANDPIPER ○
CALIDRIS BAIRDII

DATE_____

LOCATION_____

NOTES_____

_____

BUFF-BREASTED SANDPIPER ○
CALIDRIS SUBRUFICOLLIS

DATE_____

LOCATION_____

NOTES_____

_____

PURPLE SANDPIPER ○
CALIDRIS MARITIMA

DATE_____

LOCATION_____

NOTES_____

_____

ROCK SANDPIPER ○
CALIDRIS PTILOCNEMIS

DATE_____

LOCATION_____

NOTES_____

_____

STILT SANDPIPER ○
CALIDRIS HIMANTOPUS

DATE_____

LOCATION_____

NOTES_____

_____

CURLEW SANDPIPER (R) ○
CALIDRIS FERRUGINEA

DATE_____

LOCATION_____

NOTES_____

_____

RUDDY TURNSTONE ○
ARENARIA INTERPRES

DATE_____

LOCATION_____

NOTES_____

_____

BLACK TURNSTONE ○
ARENARIA MELANOCEPHALA

DATE_____

LOCATION_____

NOTES_____

_____

SURFBIRD ○
APHRIZA VIRGATTA

DATE_____

LOCATION_____

NOTES_____

_____

SPOTTED SANDPIPER ○
ACTITIS MACULARIA

DATE_____

LOCATION_____

NOTES_____

_____

SOLITARY SANDPIPER ○
TRINGA SOLITARIA

DATE_____

LOCATION_____

NOTES_____

_____

LESSER YELLOWLEGS ○
TRINGA FLAVIPES

DATE_____

LOCATION_____

NOTES_____

_____

GREATER YELLOWLEGS ○
TRINGA MELANOLEUCA

DATE_____

LOCATION_____

NOTES_____

_____

SPOTTED REDSHANK (R) ○
TRINGA ERYTHROPUS

DATE_____

LOCATION_____

NOTES_____

_____

WOOD SANDPIPER (R) ○
TRINGA GLAREOLA

DATE_____

LOCATION_____

NOTES_____

_____

TEREK SANDPIPER (R) ○
XENUS CINEREUS

DATE_____

LOCATION_____

NOTES_____

_____

WANDERING TATTLER ○
HETEROSCELUS INCANUS

DATE_____

LOCATION_____

NOTES_____

_____

GRAY-TAILED TATTLER (R) ○
HETEROSCELUS BREVIPES

DATE_____

LOCATION_____

NOTES_____

_____

COMMON SNIPE ○
GALLINAGO GALLINAGO

DATE_____

LOCATION_____

NOTES_____

_____

AMERICAN WOODCOCK ○
SCOLOPAX MINOR

DATE_____

LOCATION_____

NOTES_____

_____

LONG-BILLED DOWITCHER ○
LIMNODROMUS SCOLOPACEUS

DATE_____

LOCATION_____

NOTES_____

_____

SHORT-BILLED DOWITCHER ○
LIMNODROMUS GRISEUS

DATE_____

LOCATION_____

NOTES_____

_____

WILLET ○
CATOPTROPHORUS SEMIPALMATUS

DATE_____

LOCATION_____

NOTES_____

_____

RUFF (R) ○
PHILOMACHUS PUGNAX

DATE_____

LOCATION_____

NOTES_____

_____

UPLAND SANDPIPER ○
BARTRAMIA LONGICAUDA

DATE_____

LOCATION_____

NOTES_____

_____

MARBLED GODWIT ○
LIMOSA FEDOA

DATE_____

LOCATION_____

NOTES_____

_____

HUDSONIAN GODWIT ○
LIMOSA HAEMASTICA

DATE_____

LOCATION_____

NOTES_____

_____

BAR-TAILED GODWIT ○
LIMOSA LAPPONICA

DATE_____

LOCATION_____

NOTES_____

_____

WHIMBREL ○
NUMENIUS PHAEOPUS

DATE_____

LOCATION_____

NOTES_____

_____

BRISTLE-THIGHED CURLEW (R) ○
NUMENIUS TAHITIENSIS

DATE_____

LOCATION_____

NOTES_____

_____

LONG-BILLED CURLEW ○
NUMENIUS AMERICANUS

DATE_____

LOCATION_____

NOTES_____

_____

PHALAROPODINAE
(PHALAROPES)

WILSON'S PHALAROPE ○
PHALAROPUS TRICOLOR

DATE_____

LOCATION_____

NOTES_____

_____

RED-NECKED PHALAROPE ○
PHALAROPUS LOBATUS

DATE_____

LOCATION_____

NOTES_____

_____

RED PHALAROPE ○
PHALAROPUS FULICARIA

DATE_____

LOCATION_____

NOTES_____

_____

LARIDAE
LARINAE
(GULLS)

HERRING GULL ○
LARUS ARGENTATUS

DATE_____

LOCATION_____

NOTES_____

_____

RING-BILLED GULL ○
LARUS DELAWARENSIS

DATE_____

LOCATION_____

NOTES_____

_____

CALIFORNIA GULL ○
LARUS CALIFORNICUS

DATE_____

LOCATION_____

NOTES_____

_____

MEW GULL ○
LARUS CANUS

DATE_____

LOCATION_____

NOTES_____

_____

WESTERN GULL ○
LARUS OCCIDENTALIS

DATE_____

LOCATION_____

NOTES_____

_____

GREAT BLACK-BACKED GULL ○
LARUS MARINUS

DATE_____

LOCATION_____

NOTES_____

_____

LESSER BLACK-BACKED GULL (R) ○
LARUS FUSCUS

DATE_____

LOCATION_____

NOTES_____

_____

YELLOW-FOOTED GULL (R) ○
LARUS LIVENS

DATE_____

LOCATION_____

NOTES_____

_____

SLATY-BACKED GULL (R) ○
LARUS SCHISTISAGUS

DATE_____

LOCATION_____

NOTES_____

_____

GLAUCUS-WINGED GULL ○
LARUS GLAUCESCENS

DATE_____

LOCATION_____

NOTES_____

_____

GLAUCOUS GULL ○
LARUS HYPERBOREUS

DATE_____

LOCATION_____

NOTES_____

_____

ICELAND GULL ○
LARUS GLAUCOIDES

DATE_____

LOCATION_____

NOTES_____

_____

THAYER'S GULL ○
LARUS THAYERI

DATE_____

LOCATION_____

NOTES_____

_____

LAUGHING GULL ○
LARUS ATRICILLA

DATE_____

LOCATION_____

NOTES_____

_____

BONAPARTE'S GULL ○
LARUS PHILADELPHIA

DATE_____

LOCATION_____

NOTES_____

_____

FRANKLIN'S GULL ○
LARUS PIPIXCAN

DATE_____

LOCATION_____

NOTES_____

_____

BLACK-HEADED GULL (R) ○
LARUS RIDIBUNDUS

DATE_____

LOCATION_____

NOTES_____

_____

LITTLE GULL (R) ○
LARUS MINUTUS

DATE_____

LOCATION_____

NOTES_____

_____

HEERMANN'S GULL ○
LARUS HEERMANNI

DATE_____

LOCATION_____

NOTES_____

_____

BLACK-LEGGED KITTIWAKE ○
RISSA TRIDACTYLA

DATE_____

LOCATION_____

NOTES_____

_____

RED-LEGGED KITTIWAKE (R) ○
RISSA BREVIROSTRIS

DATE_____

LOCATION_____

NOTES_____

_____

SABINE'S GULL ○
XEMA SABINI

DATE_____

LOCATION_____

NOTES_____

_____

ROSS'S GULL (R) ○
RHODOSTETHIA ROSEA

DATE_____

LOCATION_____

NOTES_____

_____

IVORY GULL (R) ○
PAGOPHILA EBURNEA

DATE_____

LOCATION_____

NOTES_____

_____

STERNINAE
(TERNS)

FORSTER'S TERN ○
STERNA FORSTERI

DATE_____

LOCATION_____

NOTES_____

_____

COMMON TERN ○
STERNA HIRUNDO

DATE_____

LOCATION_____

NOTES_____

_____

ARCTIC TERN ○
STERNA PARADISAEA

DATE_____

LOCATION_____

NOTES_____

_____

ROSEATE TERN ○
STERNA DOUGALLII

DATE_____

LOCATION_____

NOTES_____

_____

CASPIAN TERN ○
STERNA CASPIA

DATE_____

LOCATION_____

NOTES_____

_____

ROYAL TERN ○
STERNA MAXIMA

DATE_____

LOCATION_____

NOTES_____

_____

ELEGANT TERN ○
STERNA ELEGANS

DATE_____

LOCATION_____

NOTES_____

_____

SANDWICH TERN ○
STERNA SANDVICENSIS

DATE_____

LOCATION_____

NOTES_____

_____

SOOTY TERN ○
STERNA FUSCATA

DATE_____

LOCATION_____

NOTES_____

BRIDLED TERN ○
STERNA ANAETHETUS

DATE_____

LOCATION_____

NOTES_____

ALEUTIAN TERN ○
STERNA ALEUTICA

DATE_____

LOCATION_____

NOTES_____

LEAST TERN ○
STERNA ANTILLARUM

DATE_____

LOCATION_____

NOTES_____

GULL-BILLED TERN ○
STERNA NILOTICA

DATE_____

LOCATION_____

NOTES_____

BROWN NODDY ○
ANOUS STOLIDUS

DATE_____

LOCATION_____

NOTES_____

BLACK NODDY (R) ○
ANOUS MINUTUS

DATE_____

LOCATION_____

NOTES_____

BLACK TERN ○
CHLIDONIAS NIGER

DATE_____

LOCATION_____

NOTES_____

WHITE-WINGED TERN (R) ○
CHLIDONIAS LEUCOPTERUS

DATE_____

LOCATION_____

NOTES_____

RYNCHOPINAE
(SKIMMERS)

BLACK SKIMMER ○
RYNCHOPS NIGER

DATE_____

LOCATION_____

NOTES_____

STERCORIDAE
(SKUAS & JAEGERS)

PARASITIC JAEGER ○
STERCORARIUS PARASITICUS

DATE_____

LOCATION_____

NOTES_____

LONG-TAILED JAEGER ○
STERCORARIUS LONGICAUDUS

DATE_____

LOCATION_____

NOTES_____

_____

POMARINE JAEGER ○
STERCORARIUS POMARINUS

DATE_____

LOCATION_____

NOTES_____

_____

SOUTH POLAR SKUA (R) ○
STERCORARIUS MACCORMICKI

DATE_____

LOCATION_____

NOTES_____

_____

GREAT SKUA ○
STERCORARIUS SKUA

DATE_____

LOCATION_____

NOTES_____

_____

PROCELLARIIFORMES
(PELAGIC BIRDS)
DIOMEDEIDAE
(ALBATROSS)

BLACK-FOOTED ALBATROSS ○
PHOEBASTRIA NIGRIPES

DATE_____

LOCATION_____

NOTES_____

_____

LAYSAN ALBATROSS (R) ○
PHOEBASTRIA IMMUTABILIS

DATE_____

LOCATION_____

NOTES_____

_____

PROCELLARIIDAE
(PETRELS &
SHEARWATERS)

SOOTY SHEARWATER ○
PUFFINUS GRISEUS

DATE_____

LOCATION_____

NOTES_____

_____

SHORT-TAILED SHEARWATER ○
PUFFINUS TENUIROSTRIS

DATE_____

LOCATION_____

NOTES_____

_____

FLESH-FOOTED SHEARWATER (R) ○
PUFFINUS CARNEIPES

DATE_____

LOCATION_____

NOTES_____

_____

AUDUBON SHEARWATER ○
PUFFINUS IHERMINIERI

DATE_____

LOCATION_____

NOTES_____

_____

MANX SHEARWATER ○
PUFFINUS PUFFINUS

DATE_____

LOCATION_____

NOTES_____

_____

GREATER SHEARWATER ○
PUFFINUS GRAVIS

DATE_____

LOCATION_____

NOTES_____

_____

PINK-FOOTED SHEARWATER ○
PUFFINUS CREATOPUS

DATE_____

LOCATION_____

NOTES_____

_____

BULLER'S SHEARWATER ○
PUFFINUS BULLERI

DATE_____

LOCATION_____

NOTES_____

_____

BLACK-VENTED SHEARWATER ○
PUFFINUS OPISTHOMELAS

DATE_____

LOCATION_____

NOTES_____

_____

BLACK-CAPPED PETREL ○
PTERODROMA HASITATA

DATE_____

LOCATION_____

NOTES_____

_____

NORTHERN FULMAR ○
FULMARUS GLACIALIS

DATE_____

LOCATION_____

NOTES_____

_____

CORY'S SHEARWATER ○
CALONECTRIS DIOMEDEA

DATE_____

LOCATION_____

NOTES_____

_____

WILSON'S STORM PETREL ○
OCEANICUS OCEANICUS

DATE_____

LOCATION_____

NOTES_____

_____

LEACH'S STORM PETREL ○
OCEANODROMA LEUCORHOA

DATE_____

LOCATION_____

NOTES_____

_____

BAND-RUMPED STORM PETREL ○
OCEANODROMA CASTRO

DATE_____

LOCATION_____

NOTES_____

_____

ASHY STORM PETREL ○
OCEANODROMA HOMOCHROA

DATE_____

LOCATION_____

NOTES_____

_____

BLACK STORM PETREL ○
OCEANODROMA MELANIA

DATE

LOCATION

NOTES

LEAST STORM PETREL ○
OCEANODROMA MICROSOMA

DATE

LOCATION

NOTES

FORK-TAILED
STORM PETREL ○
OCEANODROMA FURCATA

DATE

LOCATION

NOTES

WHITE-FACED
STORM PETREL ○
PELAGODROMA MARINA

DATE

LOCATION

NOTES

PHOENICOPTERIFORMES
(FLAMINGOS)

PHEONICOPTERIDAE

GREATER FLAMINGO ○
PHOENICOPTERUS RUBER

DATE

LOCATION

NOTES

CICONIIFORMES
(WADING BIRDS)
THRESKIORNITHIDAE
PLATALEINAE
(SPOONBILL)

ROSEATTE SPOONBILL ○
AJAIA AJAJA

DATE

LOCATION

NOTES

THRESKIORNITHINAE
(IBIS)

GLOSSY IBIS ○
PLEGADIS FALCINELLUS

DATE

LOCATION

NOTES

WHITE-FACED IBIS ○
PLEGADIS CHIHI

DATE

LOCATION

NOTES

WHITE IBIS ○
EUDOCIMUS ALBUS

DATE

LOCATION

NOTES

ARDEIDAE
(HERONS, EGRETS, & BITTERNS)

GREAT BLUE HERON ○
ARDEA HERODIAS

DATE_____

LOCATION_____

NOTES_____

_____

GREAT WHITE HERON ○
ARDEA HERODIAS

DATE_____

LOCATION_____

NOTES_____

_____

SNOWY EGRET ○
EGRETTA THULA

DATE_____

LOCATION_____

NOTES_____

_____

CATTLE EGRET ○
BULBUCUS IBIS

DATE_____

LOCATION_____

NOTES_____

_____

GREAT EGRET ○
ARDEA ALBA

DATE_____

LOCATION_____

NOTES_____

_____

LITTLE BLUE HERON ○
EGRETTA CAERULEA

DATE_____

LOCATION_____

NOTES_____

_____

TRICOLORED HERON ○
EGRETTA TRICOLOR

DATE_____

LOCATION_____

NOTES_____

_____

REDDISH EGRET ○
EGRETTA RUFESCENS

DATE_____

LOCATION_____

NOTES_____

_____

BLACK-CROWNED NIGHT HERON ○
NYCTICORAX NYCTICORAX

DATE_____

LOCATION_____

NOTES_____

_____

YELLOW-CROWNED NIGHT HERON ○
NYCTANASSA VIOLACEA

DATE_____

LOCATION_____

NOTES_____

_____

GREEN HERON ○
BUTORIDES VIRESCENS

DATE_____

LOCATION_____

NOTES_____

_____

AMERICAN BITTERN ○
BOTAURUS LENTIGINOSUS

DATE_____

LOCATION_____

NOTES_____

_____

LEAST BITTERN ○
IXOBRYCHUS EXILIS

DATE_____

LOCATION_____

NOTES_____

_____

CICONIIDAE
(STORKS)

WOOD STORK ○
MYCTERIA AMERICANA

DATE_____

LOCATION_____

NOTES_____

_____

CATHARTIDAE
(VULTURES)

CALIFORNIA CONDOR (R) ○
GYMNOGYPS CALIFORNIANUS

DATE_____

LOCATION_____

NOTES_____

_____

TURKEY VULTURE ○
CATHARTES AURA

DATE_____

LOCATION_____

NOTES_____

_____

BLACK VULTURE ○
CORAGYPS ATRATUS

DATE_____

LOCATION_____

NOTES_____

_____

FALCONIFORMES
ACCIPITRINAE
(HAWKS, EAGLES,
& KITES)

RED-TAILED HAWK ○
BUTEO JAMIACENSIS

DATE_____

LOCATION_____

NOTES_____

_____

ROUGH-LEGGED HAWK ○
BUTEO LAGOPUS

DATE_____

LOCATION_____

NOTES_____

_____

FERRUGINOUS HAWK ○
BUTEO REGALIS

DATE_____

LOCATION_____

NOTES_____

_____

BROAD-WINGED HAWK ○
BUTEO PLATYPTERUS

DATE_____

LOCATION_____

NOTES_____

_____

RED-SHOULDERED HAWK ○
BUTEO LINEATUS

DATE_____

LOCATION_____

NOTES_____

_____

SWAINSON'S HAWK ○
BUTEO SWAINSONI

DATE_____

LOCATION_____

NOTES_____

_____

WHITE-TAILED HAWK ○
BUTEO ALBICAUDATUS

DATE_____

LOCATION_____

NOTES_____

_____

SHORT-TAILED HAWK ○
BUTEO BRACHYURUS

DATE_____

LOCATION_____

NOTES_____

_____

ZONE-TAILED HAWK ○
BUTEO ALBONATATUS

DATE_____

LOCATION_____

NOTES_____

_____

GRAY HAWK ○
ASTURINA NITIDA

DATE_____

LOCATION_____

NOTES_____

_____

HARRIS'S HAWK ○
PARABUTEO UNICINCTUS

DATE_____

LOCATION_____

NOTES_____

_____

COMMON BLACK HAWK ○
BUTEOGALLUS ANTHRACINUS

DATE_____

LOCATION_____

NOTES_____

_____

NORTHERN HARRIER ○
CIRCUS CYANEUS

DATE_____

LOCATION_____

NOTES_____

_____

BALD EAGLE ○
HALIAEETUS LEUCOCEPHALUS

DATE_____

LOCATION_____

NOTES_____

_____

GOLDEN EAGLE ○
AQUILA CHRYSAETOS

DATE_____

LOCATION_____

NOTES_____

_____

MISSISSIPPI KITE ○
ICTINIA MISSISSIPPIENSIS

DATE_____

LOCATION_____

NOTES_____

_____

WHITE-TAILED KITE ○
ELANUS LEUCURUS

DATE_____

LOCATION_____

NOTES_____

_____

SWALLOW-TAILED KITE ○
ELANOIDES FORFICATUS

DATE_____

LOCATION_____

NOTES_____

_____

SNAIL KITE ○
ROSTRHAMUS SOCIABILIS

DATE_____

LOCATION_____

NOTES_____

_____

HOOK-BILLED KITE ○
CHONDROHIERAX UNCINATUS

DATE_____

LOCATION_____

NOTES_____

_____

SHARP-SHINNED HAWK ○
ACCIPITER STRIATUS

DATE_____

LOCATION_____

NOTES_____

_____

COOPER'S HAWK ○
ACCIPITER COOPERII

DATE_____

LOCATION_____

NOTES_____

_____

NORTHERN GOSHAWK ○
ACCIPITER GENTILIS

DATE_____

LOCATION_____

NOTES_____

_____

PANDIONINAE
(OSPREY)

OSPREY ○
PANDION HALIAETUS

DATE_____

LOCATION_____

NOTES_____

_____

CARACARINAE
(CARACARA)

CRESTED CARACARA ○
CARACARA CHERIWAY

DATE_____

LOCATION_____

NOTES_____

_____

FALCONINAE
(FALCONS)

AMERICAN KESTREL ○
FALCO SPARVERIUS

DATE_____

LOCATION_____

NOTES_____

_____

MERLIN ○
FALCO COLUMBARIUS

DATE_____

LOCATION_____

NOTES_____

_____

APLOMADO FALCON (R) ○
FALCO FEMORALIS

DATE_____

LOCATION_____

NOTES_____

_____

PEREGRINE FALCON ○
FALCO PEREGRINUS

DATE_____

LOCATION_____

NOTES_____

_____

PRAIRIE FALCON ○
FALCO MEXICANUS

DATE_____

LOCATION_____

NOTES_____

_____

GYRFALCON ○
FALCO RUSTICOLUS

DATE_____

LOCATION_____

NOTES_____

_____

STRIGIFORMES
(OWLS)
STRIGIDAE

GREAT HORNED OWL ○
BUBO VIRGINIANUS

DATE_____

LOCATION_____

NOTES_____

_____

LONG-EARED OWL ○
ASIO OTUS

DATE_____

LOCATION_____

NOTES_____

_____

SHORT-EARED OWL ○
ASIO FLAMMEUS

DATE_____

LOCATION_____

NOTES_____

_____

EASTERN SCREECH OWL ○
OTUS ASIO

DATE_____

LOCATION_____

NOTES_____

_____

WESTERN SCREECH OWL ○
OTUS KENNICOTTII

DATE_____

LOCATION_____

NOTES_____

_____

WHISKERED SCREECH OWL ○
OTUS TRICHOPSIS

DATE_____

LOCATION_____

NOTES_____

_____

FLAMMULATED OWL ○
OTUS FLAMMEOLUS

DATE_____

LOCATION_____

NOTES_____

_____

ELF OWL ○
MICRATHENE WHITNEYI

DATE_____

LOCATION_____

NOTES_____

_____

BARRED OWL ○
STRIX VARIA

DATE_____

LOCATION_____

NOTES_____

_____

SPOTTED OWL ○
STRIX OCCIDENTALIS

DATE_____

LOCATION_____

NOTES_____

_____

GREAT GRAY OWL ○
STRIX NEBULOSA

DATE_____

LOCATION_____

NOTES_____

_____

SNOWY OWL ○
NYCTEA SCANDIACA

DATE_____

LOCATION_____

NOTES_____

_____

NORTHERN HAWK OWL ○
SURNIA ULULA

DATE_____

LOCATION_____

NOTES_____

_____

NORTHERN SAW-WHET OWL ○
AEGOLIUS ACADICUS

DATE_____

LOCATION_____

NOTES_____

_____

BOREAL OWL ○
AEGOLIUS FUNEREUS

DATE_____

LOCATION_____

NOTES_____

_____

BURROWING OWL ○
ATHENE CUNICULARIA

DATE_____

LOCATION_____

NOTES_____

_____

NORTHERN PYGMY OWL ○
GLAUCIDIUM GNOMA

DATE_____

LOCATION_____

NOTES_____

_____

FERRUGINOUS PYGMY OWL (R) ○
GLAUCIDIUM BRASILIANUM

DATE_____

LOCATION_____

NOTES_____

_____

TYTONIDAE
(BARN OWLS)

BARN OWL ○
TYTO ALBA

DATE_____

LOCATION_____

NOTES_____

_____

GALLIFORMES
(CHICKEN-LIKE BIRDS)
CRACIDAE
(CHACHALACAS)

PLAIN CHACHALACA ○
ORTALIS VETULA

DATE_____

LOCATION_____

NOTES_____

_____

PHASIANIDAE
PHASIANAE
(PHEASANTS)

RING-NECKED PHEASANT (I) ○
PHASIANUS COLCHICUS

DATE_____

LOCATION_____

NOTES_____

_____

GRAY PARTRIDGE (I) ○
PERDIX PERDIX

DATE_____

LOCATION_____

NOTES_____

_____

HIMALAYAN SNOWCOCK (I) (R) ○
TETRAOGALLUS HIMALAYENSIS

DATE_____

LOCATION_____

NOTES_____

_____

CHUKAR (I) ○
ALECTORIS CHUKAR

DATE_____

LOCATION_____

NOTES_____

_____

TETRAONINAE
(GROUSE)

RUFFED GROUSE ○
BONASA UMBELLUS

DATE_____

LOCATION_____

NOTES_____

_____

SPRUCE GROUSE ○
FALCIPENNIS CANADENSIS

DATE_____

LOCATION_____

NOTES_____

_____

BLUE GROUSE ○
DENDRAGAPUS OBSCURUS

DATE_____

LOCATION_____

NOTES_____

_____

WILLOW PTARMIGAN ⭘
LAGOPUS LAGOPUS

DATE_____

LOCATION_____

NOTES_____

_____

WHITE-TAILED PTARMIGAN ⭘
LAGOPUS LEUCURUS

DATE_____

LOCATION_____

NOTES_____

_____

ROCK PTARMIGAN ⭘
LAGOPUS MUTUS

DATE_____

LOCATION_____

NOTES_____

_____

GREATER SAGE GROUSE ⭘
CENTROCERCUS UROPHASIANUS

DATE_____

LOCATION_____

NOTES_____

_____

GUNNISON SAGE GROUSE ⭘
CENTROCERCUS MINIMUS

DATE_____

LOCATION_____

NOTES_____

_____

GREATER PRAIRIE CHICKEN ⭘
TYMPANUCHUS CUPIDO

DATE_____

LOCATION_____

NOTES_____

_____

LESSER PRAIRIE CHICKEN ⭘
TYMPANUCHUS PALLIDICINCTUS

DATE_____

LOCATION_____

NOTES_____

_____

SHARP-TAILED GROUSE ⭘
TYMPANUCHUS PHASIANELLUS

DATE_____

LOCATION_____

NOTES_____

_____

MELEAGRIDINAE
(TURKEYS)

WILD TURKEY ⭘
MELEAGRIS GALLOPAVO

DATE_____

LOCATION_____

NOTES_____

_____

ODONTOPHORIDAE
(QUAIL)

BOBWHITE ⭘
COLINUS VIRGINIANUS

DATE_____

LOCATION_____

NOTES_____

_____

MONTEZUMA QUAIL ⭘
CYRTONYX MONTEZUMA

DATE_____

LOCATION_____

NOTES_____

_____

CALIFORNIA QUAIL ○
CALLIPEPLA CALIFORNICA

DATE_____

LOCATION_____

NOTES_____

_____

GAMBEL'S QUAIL ○
CALLIPEPLA GAMBELII

DATE_____

LOCATION_____

NOTES_____

_____

SCALED QUAIL ○
CALLIPEPLA SQUAMATA

DATE_____

LOCATION_____

NOTES_____

_____

MOUNTAIN QUAIL ○
OREORTYX PICTUS

DATE_____

LOCATION_____

NOTES_____

_____

COLUMBIFORMES
(PIGEONS & DOVES)
COLUMBIDAE

MOURNING DOVE ○
ZENAIDA MACROURA

DATE_____

LOCATION_____

NOTES_____

_____

WHITE-WINGED DOVE ○
ZENAIDA ASIATICA

DATE_____

LOCATION_____

NOTES_____

_____

RINGED TURTLE DOVE (I) ○
STREPTOPELIA RISORIA

DATE_____

LOCATION_____

NOTES_____

_____

EURASIAN COLLARED DOVE (I) ○
STREPTOPELIA DECAOCTO

DATE_____

LOCATION_____

NOTES_____

_____

SPOTTED DOVE (I) ○
STREPTOPELIA CHINENSIS

DATE_____

LOCATION_____

NOTES_____

_____

INCA DOVE ○
COLUMBINA INCA

DATE_____

LOCATION_____

NOTES_____

_____

ROCK DOVE (PIGEON) ○
COLUMBA LIVIA

DATE_____

LOCATION_____

NOTES_____

_____

BAND-TAILED PIGEON ○
COLUMBA FASCIATA

DATE_____

LOCATION_____

NOTES_____

WHITE-CROWNED PIGEON ○
COLUMBA LEUCOCEPHALA

DATE_____

LOCATION_____

NOTES_____

RED-BILLED PIGEON ○
COLUMBA FLAVIROSTRIS

DATE_____

LOCATION_____

NOTES_____

COMMON GROUND DOVE ○
COLUMBINA PASSERINA

DATE_____

LOCATION_____

NOTES_____

RUDDY GROUND DOVE (R) ○
COLUMBINA TALPACOTI

DATE_____

LOCATION_____

NOTES_____

WHITE-TIPPED DOVE (R) ○
LEPTOTILA VERREAUXI

DATE_____

LOCATION_____

NOTES_____

CUCULIFORMES
CUCULIDAE
(CUCKOOS, ROADRUNNER & ANIS)

YELLOW-BILLED CUCKOO ○
COCCYZUS AMERICANUS

DATE_____

LOCATION_____

NOTES_____

BLACK-BILLED CUCKOO ○
COCCYZUS ERYTHROPTHALMUS

DATE_____

LOCATION_____

NOTES_____

MANGROVE CUCKOO ○
COCCYZUS MINOR

DATE_____

LOCATION_____

NOTES_____

COMMON CUCKOO (R) ○
CUCULUS CANORUS

DATE_____

LOCATION_____

NOTES_____

GREATER ROADRUNNER ○
GEOCOCCYX CALIFORNIANUS

DATE_____

LOCATION_____

NOTES_____

GROOVE-BILLED ANI ○
CROTOPHAGA SULCIROSTRIS

DATE_____

LOCATION_____

NOTES_____

_____

SMOOTH-BILLED ANI (R) ○
CROTOPHAGA ANI

DATE_____

LOCATION_____

NOTES_____

_____

PSITTACIFORMES
(PARROTS)
PSITTACIDAE

BUDGERIGAR (I) ○
MELOPSITTACUS UNDULATUS

DATE_____

LOCATION_____

NOTES_____

_____

COCKATIEL (I) ○
NYMPHICUS HOLLANDICUS

DATE_____

LOCATION_____

NOTES_____

_____

PLATYCERECINAE & PSITTACINAE

ROSE-RINGED PARAKEET (I) ○
PSITTACULA KRAMERI

DATE_____

LOCATION_____

NOTES_____

_____

PEACH-FACED LOVEBIRD (I) ○
AGAPORNIS ROSEICOLLIS

DATE_____

LOCATION_____

NOTES_____

_____

ARINAE
(NEW WORLD PARROTS)

BLACK-HOODED PARAKEET (I) ○
NANDAYUS NENDAY

DATE_____

LOCATION_____

NOTES_____

_____

MONK PARAKEET (I) ○
MYIOPSITTA MONACHUS

DATE_____

LOCATION_____

NOTES_____

_____

YELLOW-CHEVRONED PARAKEET (I) ○
BROTOGERIS CHIRIRI

DATE_____

LOCATION_____

NOTES_____

_____

WHITE-WINGED PARAKEET (I) ○
BROTOGERIS VERSICOLURUS

DATE_____

LOCATION_____

NOTES_____

_____

THICK-BILLED PARROT (I) ○
RHYNCHOPSITTA PACHYRHYNCHA

DATE_____

LOCATION_____

NOTES_____

_____

RED-CROWNED PARROT (I) ○
AMAZONA VIRIDIGENALIS

DATE_____

LOCATION_____

NOTES_____

_____

YELLOW-HEADED PARROT (I) ○
AMAZONA ORATRIX

DATE_____

LOCATION_____

NOTES_____

_____

LILAC-CROWNED PARROT (I) ○
AMAZONA FINSCHI

DATE_____

LOCATION_____

NOTES_____

_____

BLUE-CROWNED PARAKEET (I) ○
ARATINGA ACUTICAUDATA

DATE_____

LOCATION_____

NOTES_____

_____

GREEN PARAKEET (I) ○
ARATINGA HOLOCHLORA

DATE_____

LOCATION_____

NOTES_____

_____

MITRED PARAKEET (I) ○
ARATINGA MITRATA

DATE_____

LOCATION_____

NOTES_____

_____

RED-MASKED PARAKEET (I) ○
ARATINGA ERYTHROGENYS

DATE_____

LOCATION_____

NOTES_____

CAPRIMULGIFORMES
(NIGHTJARS)
CAPRIMULGIDAE
CHORDEILINAE
(NIGHTHAWKS)

COMMON NIGHTHAWK ○
CHORDEILES MINOR

DATE_____

LOCATION_____

NOTES_____

_____

LESSER NIGHTHAWK ○
CHORDEILES ACUTIPENNIS

DATE_____

LOCATION_____

NOTES_____

_____

ANTILLEAN NIGHTHAWK ○
CHORDEILES GUNDLACHII

DATE_____

LOCATION_____

NOTES_____

_____

CAPRIMULGINAE
(POORWILLS)

COMMON PARAQUE ○
NYCTIDROMUS ALBICOLLIS

DATE_____

LOCATION_____

NOTES_____

_____

WHIP-POOR-WILL ○
CAPRIMULGUS VOCIFERUS

DATE_____

LOCATION_____

NOTES_____

_____

CHUCK-WILL'S WIDOW ○
CAPRIMULGUS CAROLINENSIS

DATE_____

LOCATION_____

NOTES_____

_____

BUFF-COLLARED
NIGHTJAR (R) ○
CAPRIMULGUS RIDGWAYI

DATE_____

LOCATION_____

NOTES_____

_____

COMMON POORWILL ○
PHALAENOPTILUS NUTTALLII

DATE_____

LOCATION_____

NOTES_____

_____

APODIFORMES
APODIDAE
(SWIFTS)
CYPSELOIDINAE

BLACK SWIFT ○
CYPSELOIDES NIGER

DATE_____

LOCATION_____

NOTES_____

_____

CHAETURINAE
& APODINAE

CHIMNEY SWIFT ○
CHAETURA PELAGICA

DATE_____

LOCATION_____

NOTES_____

_____

VAUX'S SWIFT ○
CHAETURA VAUXI

DATE_____

LOCATION_____

NOTES_____

_____

WHITE-THROATED SWIFT ○
AERONAUTES SAXATALIS

DATE_____

LOCATION_____

NOTES_____

_____

GALLERY OF

NORTH AMERICAN BIRDS

BALD EAGLE
page 33

BALTIMORE ORIOLE
page 77

BARN SWALLOW
page 56

BLACK-BILLED MAGPIE
page 64

BLUE-GRAY GNATCATCHER
page 68

BLUE JAY
page 64

BREWER'S BLACKBIRD
page 77

CAROLINA CHICKADEE
page 65

CAROLINA WREN
page 67

COMMON MERGANSER
page 12

COMMON REDPOLL
page 83

COMMON YELLOWTHROAT
page 74

DOUBLE-CRESTED CORMORANT
page 15

EASTERN PHOEBE
page 56

EASTERN BLUEBIRD
page 60

EASTERN SCREECH OWL
page 35

GOLDEN EAGLE
page 33

GOLDFINCH
page 83

GREAT BLACK-BACKED GULL
page 24

GREAT HORNED OWL
page 35

HORNED LARK
page 63

INDIGO BUNTING
page 84

NORTHERN CARDINAL
page 84

NORTHERN FLICKER
page 54

NORTHERN MOCKINGBIRD
page 62

PINE SISKIN
page 83

RED-EYED VIREO
page 70

RED-TAILED HAWK
page 32

RED-WINGED BLACKBIRD
page 76

RUBY-THROATED HUMMINGBIRD
page 51

RUFFED GROUSE
page 37

RUFOUS HUMMINGBIRD
page 51

TRICOLORED HERON
page 31

TUFTED TITMOUSE
page 66

WOOD THRUSH
page 61

YELLOW-BILLED CUCKOO
page 40

TROCHILIDAE
(HUMMINGBIRDS)

RUBY-THROATED HUMMINGBIRD ○
ARCHILOCHUS COLUBRIS

DATE_____

LOCATION_____

NOTES_____

_____

BLACK-CHINNED HUMMINGBIRD ○
ARCHILOCHUS ALEXANDRI

DATE_____

LOCATION_____

NOTES_____

_____

ANNA'S HUMMINGBIRD ○
CALYPTE ANNA

DATE_____

LOCATION_____

NOTES_____

_____

COSTA'S HUMMINGBIRD ○
CALYPTE COSTAE

DATE_____

LOCATION_____

NOTES_____

_____

BROAD-TAILED HUMMINGBIRD ○
SELASPHORUS PLATYCERCUS

DATE_____

LOCATION_____

NOTES_____

_____

RUFOUS HUMMINGBIRD ○
SELASPHORUS RUFUS

DATE_____

LOCATION_____

NOTES_____

ALLEN'S HUMMINGBIRD ○
SELASPHORUS SASIN

DATE_____

LOCATION_____

NOTES_____

CALLIOPE HUMMINGBIRD ○
STULLA CALLIOPE

DATE_____

LOCATION_____

NOTES_____

BROAD-BILLED HUMMINGBIRD ○
CYNANTHUS LATIROSTRIS

DATE_____

LOCATION_____

NOTES_____

BUFF-BELLIED HUMMINGBIRD ○
AMAZILIA YUCATANENSIS

DATE_____

LOCATION_____

NOTES_____

_____

BERRYLINE HUMMINGBIRD (R) ○
AMAZILIA BERYLLINA

DATE_____

LOCATION_____

NOTES_____

_____

VIOLET-CROWNED HUMMINGBIRD ○
AMAZILIA VIOLICEPS

DATE_____

LOCATION_____

NOTES_____

_____

BLUE-THROATED HUMMINGBIRD ○
LAMPORNIS CLEMENCIAE

DATE_____

LOCATION_____

NOTES_____

_____

MAGNIFICENT HUMMINGBIRD ○
EUGENES FULGENS

DATE_____

LOCATION_____

NOTES_____

_____

LUCIFER HUMMINGBIRD ○
CALOTHORAX LUCIFER

DATE_____

LOCATION_____

NOTES_____

_____

WHITE-EARED HUMMINGBIRD (R) ○
HYLOCHARIS LEUCOTIS

DATE_____

LOCATION_____

NOTES_____

_____

GREEN VIOLET-EAR (R) ○
COLIBRI THALASSINUS

DATE_____

LOCATION_____

NOTES_____

_____

PLAIN-CAPPED STARTHROAT (R) ○
HELIOMASTER CONSTANTII

DATE_____

LOCATION_____

NOTES_____

_____

GREEN-BREASTED MANGO (R) ○
ANTHRACOTHORAX PREVOSTII

DATE_____

LOCATION_____

NOTES_____

_____

CORACIIFORMES
ALCEDINIDAE
(KINGFISHERS)

BELTED KINGFISHER ○
CERYLE ALCYON

DATE_____

LOCATION_____

NOTES_____

_____

RINGED KINGFISHER (R) ◯
CERYLE TORQUATUS

DATE_____

LOCATION_____

NOTES_____

_____

GREEN KINGFISHER ◯
CHLOROCERYLE AMERICANA

DATE_____

LOCATION_____

NOTES_____

_____

TROGONIFORMES
TROGONIDAE
(TROGONS)

ELEGANT TROGON ◯
TROGON ELEGANS

DATE_____

LOCATION_____

NOTES_____

_____

EARED TROGON (R) ◯
EUPTILOTIS NEOXENUS

DATE_____

LOCATION_____

NOTES_____

_____

PICIFORMES
PICIDAE
(WOODPECKERS)

RED-HEADED WOODPECKER ◯
MELANERPES ERYTHROCEPHALUS

DATE_____

LOCATION_____

NOTES_____

_____

ACORN WOODPECKER ◯
MELANERPES FORMICIVORUS

DATE_____

LOCATION_____

NOTES_____

_____

LEWIS'S WOODPECKER ◯
MELANERPES LEWIS

DATE_____

LOCATION_____

NOTES_____

_____

RED-BELLIED WOODPECKER ◯
MELANERPES CAROLINENSIS

DATE_____

LOCATION_____

NOTES_____

_____

GOLDEN-FRONTED WOODPECKER ◯
MELANERPES AURIFRONS

DATE_____

LOCATION_____

NOTES_____

_____

GILA WOODPECKER ○
MELANERPES UROPYGIALIS

DATE_____

LOCATION_____

NOTES_____

_____

YELLOW-SHAFTED FLICKER ○
COLAPTES AURATUS

DATE_____

LOCATION_____

NOTES_____

_____

RED-SHAFTED FLICKER ○
COLAPTES AURATUS

DATE_____

LOCATION_____

NOTES_____

_____

GILDED FLICKER ○
COLAPTES CHRYSOIDES

DATE_____

LOCATION_____

NOTES_____

_____

WHITE-HEADED WOODPECKER ○
PICOIDES ALBOLARVATUS

DATE_____

LOCATION_____

NOTES_____

_____

NUTTALL'S WOODPECKER ○
PICOIDES NUTTALLII

DATE_____

LOCATION_____

NOTES_____

_____

LADDER-BACKED WOODPECKER ○
PICOIDES SCALARIS

DATE_____

LOCATION_____

NOTES_____

_____

DOWNY WOODPECKER ○
PICOIDES PUBESCENS

DATE_____

LOCATION_____

NOTES_____

_____

HAIRY WOODPECKER ○
PICOIDES VILLOSUS

DATE_____

LOCATION_____

NOTES_____

_____

THREE-TOED WOODPECKER ○
PICOIDES TRIDACTYLUS

DATE_____

LOCATION_____

NOTES_____

_____

BLACK-BACKED WOODPECKER ○
PICOIDES ARCTICUS

DATE_____

LOCATION_____

NOTES_____

_____

RED-COCKADED WOODPECKER ○
PICOIDES BOREALIS

DATE_____

LOCATION_____

NOTES_____

_____

ARIZONA WOODPECKER ○
PICOIDES ARIZONAE

DATE_____

LOCATION_____

NOTES_____

_____

YELLOW-BELLIED SAPSUCKER ○
SPHYRAPICUS VARIUS

DATE_____

LOCATION_____

NOTES_____

_____

RED-NAPED SAPSUCKER ○
SPHYRAPICUS NUCHALIS

DATE_____

LOCATION_____

NOTES_____

_____

RED-BREASTED SAPSUCKER ○
SPHYRAPICUS RUBER

DATE_____

LOCATION_____

NOTES_____

_____

WILLIAMSON'S SAPSUCKER ○
SPHYRAPICUS THYROIDEUS

DATE_____

LOCATION_____

NOTES_____

_____

PILEATED WOODPECKER ○
DRYOCOPUS PILEATUS

DATE_____

LOCATION_____

NOTES_____

_____

PASSERIFORMES
(PERCHING BIRDS)
HIRUNDINIDAE
(SWALLOWS)

PURPLE MARTIN ○
PROGNE SUBIS

DATE_____

LOCATION_____

NOTES_____

_____

TREE SWALLOW ○
TACHYCINETA BICOLOR

DATE_____

LOCATION_____

NOTES_____

_____

VIOLET-GREEN SWALLOW ○
TACHYCINETA THALASSINA

DATE_____

LOCATION_____

NOTES_____

_____

BAHAMA SWALLOW (R) ○
TACHYCINETA CYANEOVIRIDIS

DATE_____

LOCATION_____

NOTES_____

_____

BARN SWALLOW ○
HIRUNDO RUSTICA

DATE_____

LOCATION_____

NOTES_____

_____

CLIFF SWALLOW ○
PETROCHELIDON PYRRHONOTA

DATE_____

LOCATION_____

NOTES_____

_____

CAVE SWALLOW ○
PETROCHELIDON FULVA

DATE_____

LOCATION_____

NOTES_____

_____

BANK SWALLOW ○
RIPARIA RIPARIA

DATE_____

LOCATION_____

NOTES_____

_____

NORTHERN ROUGH-WINGED SWALLOW ○
STELGIDOPTERYX SERRIPENNIS

DATE_____

LOCATION_____

NOTES_____

_____

TYRANNIDAE
FLUVICOLINAE

OLIVE-SIDED FLYCATCHER ○
CONTOPUS COOPERI

DATE_____

LOCATION_____

NOTES_____

_____

EASTERN WOOD PEWEE ○
CONTOPUS VIRENS

DATE_____

LOCATION_____

NOTES_____

_____

WESTERN WOOD PEWEE ○
CONTOPUS SORDIDULUS

DATE_____

LOCATION_____

NOTES_____

_____

GREATER PEWEE ○
CONTOPUS PERTINAX

DATE_____

LOCATION_____

NOTES_____

_____

EASTERN PHOEBE ○
SAYORNIS PHOEBE

DATE_____

LOCATION_____

NOTES_____

_____

BLACK PHOEBE ○
SAYORNIS NIGRICANS

DATE_____

LOCATION_____

NOTES_____

_____

SAY'S PHOEBE ○
SAYORNIS SAYA

DATE_____

LOCATION_____

NOTES_____

_____

VERMILION FLYCATCHER ○
PYROCEPHALUS RUBINUS

DATE_____

LOCATION_____

NOTES_____

_____

LEAST FLYCATCHER ○
EMPIDONAX MINIMUS

DATE_____

LOCATION_____

NOTES_____

_____

**YELLOW-BELLIED
FLYCATCHER** ○
EMPIDONAX FLAVIVENTRIS

DATE_____

LOCATION_____

NOTES_____

_____

ACADIAN FLYCATCHER ○
EMPIDONAX VIRESCENS

DATE_____

LOCATION_____

NOTES_____

_____

ALDER FLYCATCHER ○
EMPIDONAX ALNORUM

DATE_____

LOCATION_____

NOTES_____

_____

WILLOW FLYCATCHER ○
EMPIDONAX TRAILLII

DATE_____

LOCATION_____

NOTES_____

_____

PACIFIC-SLOPE FLYCATCHER ○
EMPIDONAX DIFFICILIS

DATE_____

LOCATION_____

NOTES_____

_____

CORDILLERAN FLYCATCHER ○
EMPIDONAX OCCIDENTALIS

DATE_____

LOCATION_____

NOTES_____

_____

HAMMOND'S FLYCATCHER ○
EMPIDONAX HAMMONDII

DATE_____

LOCATION_____

NOTES_____

_____

DUSKY FLYCATCHER ○
EMPIDONAX OBERHOLSERI

DATE_____

LOCATION_____

NOTES_____

_____

GRAY FLYCATCHER ○
EMPIDONAX WRIGHTII

DATE_____

LOCATION_____

NOTES_____

_____

BUFF-BREASTED
FLYCATCHER ○
EMPIDONAX FULVIFRONS

DATE_____

LOCATION_____

NOTES_____

_____

TYRANNINAE

EASTERN KINGBIRD ○
TYRANNUS TYRANNUS

DATE_____

LOCATION_____

NOTES_____

_____

GRAY KINGBIRD ○
TYRANNUS DOMINICENSIS

DATE_____

LOCATION_____

NOTES_____

_____

WESTERN KINGBIRD ○
TYRANNUS VERTICALIS

DATE_____

LOCATION_____

NOTES_____

_____

CASSIN'S KINGBIRD ○
TYRANNUS VOCIFERANS

DATE_____

LOCATION_____

NOTES_____

_____

COUCH'S KINGBIRD ○
TYRANNUS COUCHII

DATE_____

LOCATION_____

NOTES_____

_____

TROPICAL KINGBIRD ○
TYRANNUS MELANCHOLICUS

DATE_____

LOCATION_____

NOTES_____

_____

THICK-BILLED KINGBIRD (R) ○
TYRANNUS CRASSIROSTRIS

DATE_____

LOCATION_____

NOTES_____

_____

SCISSOR-TAILED
FLYCATCHER ○
TYRANNUS FORFICATUS

DATE_____

LOCATION_____

NOTES_____

_____

FORK-TAILED
FLYCATCHER (R) ○
TYRANNUS SAVANA

DATE_____

LOCATION_____

NOTES_____

_____

BROWN-CRESTED
FLYCATCHER ○
MYIARCHUS TYRANNULUS

DATE_____

LOCATION_____

NOTES_____

_____

DUSKY-CAPPED
FLYCATCHER ○
MYIARCHUS TUBERECULIFER

DATE_____

LOCATION_____

NOTES_____

_____

GREAT CRESTED
FLYCATCHER ○
MYIARCHUS CRINITUS

DATE_____

LOCATION_____

NOTES_____

_____

ASH-THROATED
FLYCATCHER ○
MYIARCHUS CINERASCENS

DATE_____

LOCATION_____

NOTES_____

_____

GREAT KISKADEE ○
PITANGUS SULPHURATUS

DATE_____

LOCATION_____

NOTES_____

_____

SULPHUR-BELLIED
FLYCATCHER ○
MYIODYNASTES LUTEIVENTRIS

DATE_____

LOCATION_____

NOTES_____

_____

ROSE-THROATED BECARD ○
PACHYRAMPHUS AGLAIAE

DATE_____

LOCATION_____

NOTES_____

_____

NORTHERN BEARDLESS
TYRANNULET ○
CAMPTOSTOMA IMBERBE

DATE_____

LOCATION_____

NOTES_____

_____

TURDIDAE
(THRUSHES)

AMERICAN ROBIN ○
TURDUS MIGRATORIUS

DATE_____

LOCATION_____

NOTES_____

_____

CLAY-COLORED ROBIN (R) ○
TURDUS GRAYI

DATE_____

LOCATION_____

NOTES_____

_____

RUFOUS-BACKED ROBIN (R) ○
TURDUS RUFOPALLIATUS

DATE_____

LOCATION_____

NOTES_____

_____

FIELDFARE (R) ○
TURDUS PILARIS

DATE_____

LOCATION_____

NOTES_____

_____

EYEBROWED THRUSH (R) ○
TURDUS OBSCURUS

DATE_____

LOCATION_____

NOTES_____

_____

DUSKY THRUSH (R) ○
TURDUS NAUMANNI

DATE_____

LOCATION_____

NOTES_____

_____

AZTEC THRUSH (R) ○
RIDGWAYIA PINICOLA

DATE_____

LOCATION_____

NOTES_____

_____

NORTHERN WHEATEATER ○
OENANTHE OENANTHE

DATE_____

LOCATION_____

NOTES_____

_____

BLUETHROAT ○
LUSCINIA SVECICA

DATE_____

LOCATION_____

NOTES_____

_____

EASTERN BLUEBIRD ○
SIALIA MEXICANA

DATE_____

LOCATION_____

NOTES_____

_____

WESTERN BLUEBIRD ○
SIALIA SIALIS

DATE_____

LOCATION_____

NOTES_____

_____

MOUNTAIN BLUEBIRD ○
SIALIA CURRUCOIDES

DATE_____

LOCATION_____

NOTES_____

_____

TOWNSEND'S SOLITAIRE ○
MYADESTES TOWNSENDI

DATE_____

LOCATION_____

NOTES_____

_____

VARIED THRUSH ○
IXOEUS NAEVIUS

DATE_____

LOCATION_____

NOTES_____

_____

HERMIT THRUSH ○
CATHARUS GUTTATUS

DATE_____

LOCATION_____

NOTES_____

_____

VEERY ○
CATHARUS FUSCESCENS

DATE_____

LOCATION_____

NOTES_____

_____

GRAY-CHEEKED THRUSH ○
CATHARUS MINIMUS

DATE_____

LOCATION_____

NOTES_____

_____

BICKNELL'S THRUSH ○
CATHARUS BICKNELLI

DATE_____

LOCATION_____

NOTES_____

_____

WOOD THRUSH ○
HYLOCICHLA MUSTELINA

DATE_____

LOCATION_____

NOTES_____

_____

SWAINSON'S THRUSH ○
CATHARUS USTULATUS

DATE_____

LOCATION_____

NOTES_____

_____

MIMIDAE
(THRASHERS)

BROWN THRASHER ○
TOXOSTOMA RUFUM

DATE_____

LOCATION_____

NOTES_____

_____

LONG-BILLED THRASHER ○
TOXOSTOMA LONGIROSTRE

DATE_____

LOCATION_____

NOTES_____

_____

CURVE-BILLED THRASHER ○
TOXOSTOMA CURVIROSTRE

DATE_____

LOCATION_____

NOTES_____

_____

BENDIRE'S THRASHER ○
TOXOSTOMA BENDIREI

DATE_____

LOCATION_____

NOTES_____

_____

CALIFORNIA THRASHER ○
TOXOSTOMA REDIVIVUM

DATE_____

LOCATION_____

NOTES_____

_____

CRISSAL THRASHER ○
TOXOSTOMA CRISSALE

DATE_____

LOCATION_____

NOTES_____

_____

LE CONTE'S THRASHER ○
TOXOSTOMA LECONTEI

DATE_____

LOCATION_____

NOTES_____

_____

SAGE THRASHER ○
OREOSCOPTES MONTANUS

DATE_____

LOCATION_____

NOTES_____

_____

GRAY CATBIRD ○
DUMETELA CAROLINENSIS

DATE_____

LOCATION_____

NOTES_____

_____

NORTHERN MOCKINGBIRD ○
MIMUS POLYGLOTTOS

DATE_____

LOCATION_____

NOTES_____

_____

BAHAMA MOCKINGBIRD (R) ○
MIMUS GUNDLACHII

DATE_____

LOCATION_____

NOTES_____

_____

LANIDAE
(S H R I K E S)

NORTHERN SHRIKE ○
LANIUS EXCUBITOR

DATE_____

LOCATION_____

NOTES_____

_____

LOGGERHEAD SHRIKE ○
LANIUS LUDOVICIANUS

DATE_____

LOCATION_____

NOTES_____

_____

PTILOGONATIDAE
(S I L K Y   F L Y C A T C H E R S)

PHAINOPEPLA ○
PHAINOPEPLA NITENS

DATE_____

LOCATION_____

NOTES_____

_____

BOMBYCILLIDAE
(W A X W I N G S)

CEDAR WAXWING ○
BOMBYCILLA CEDRORUM

DATE_____

LOCATION_____

NOTES_____

_____

BOHEMIAN WAXWING ○
BOMBYCILLA GARRULUS

DATE_____

LOCATION_____

NOTES_____

_____

PYCNONOTIDAE
(BULBULS)

RED-WHISKERED BULBUL (I) ○
PYCNONOTUS JOCOSUS

DATE_____

LOCATION_____

NOTES_____

_____

ALAUDIDAE
(LARKS)

HORNED LARK ○
EREMOPHILA ALPESTRIS

DATE_____

LOCATION_____

NOTES_____

_____

SKY LARK (I) ○
ALAUDA ARVENSIS

DATE_____

LOCATION_____

NOTES_____

_____

MOTACILLIDAE
(WAGTAILS)

YELLOW WAGTAIL ○
MOTACILLA FLAVA

DATE_____

LOCATION_____

NOTES_____

_____

WHITE WAGTAIL ○
MOTACILLA ALBA

DATE_____

LOCATION_____

NOTES_____

_____

BLACK-BACKED WAGTAIL (R) ○
MOTACILLA LUGENS

DATE_____

LOCATION_____

NOTES_____

_____

RED-THROATED PIPIT (R) ○
ANTHUS CERVINUS

DATE_____

LOCATION_____

NOTES_____

_____

AMERICAN PIPIT ○
ANTHUS RUBESCENS

DATE_____

LOCATION_____

NOTES_____

_____

SPRAGUE'S PIPIT ○
ANTHUS SPRAGUEII

DATE_____

LOCATION_____

NOTES_____

_____

CINCLIDAE
(DIPPERS)

AMERICAN DIPPER ○
CINCLUS MEXICANUS

DATE_____

LOCATION_____

NOTES_____

_____

CORVIDAE
(JAYS & CROWS)

BLUE JAY ○
CYANOCITTA CRISTATA

DATE_____

LOCATION_____

NOTES_____

_____

STELLER'S JAY ○
CYANOCITTA STELLERI

DATE_____

LOCATION_____

NOTES_____

_____

GREEN JAY ○
CYANOCORAX YNCAS

DATE_____

LOCATION_____

NOTES_____

_____

BROWN JAY (R) ○
CYANOCORAX MORIO

DATE_____

LOCATION_____

NOTES_____

_____

FLORIDA SCRUB JAY ○
APHELOCOMA COERULESCENS

DATE_____

LOCATION_____

NOTES_____

_____

ISLAND SCRUB JAY (R) ○
APHELOCOMA INSULARIS

DATE_____

LOCATION_____

NOTES_____

_____

WESTERN SCRUB JAY ○
APHELOCOMA CALIFORNICA

DATE_____

LOCATION_____

NOTES_____

_____

MEXICAN JAY
APHELOCOMA ULTRAMARINA

DATE_____

LOCATION_____

NOTES_____

_____

BLACK-BILLED MAGPIE ○
PICA HUDSONIA

DATE_____

LOCATION_____

NOTES_____

_____

YELLOW-BILLED MAGPIE ◯
PICA NUTTALLI

DATE_____

LOCATION_____

NOTES_____

_____

GRAY JAY ◯
PERISOREUS CANADENSIS

DATE_____

LOCATION_____

NOTES_____

_____

PINYON JAY ◯
GYMNORHINUS CYANOCEPHALUS

DATE_____

LOCATION_____

NOTES_____

_____

CLARK'S NUTCRACKER ◯
NUCIFRAGA COLUMBIANA

DATE_____

LOCATION_____

NOTES_____

_____

AMERICAN CROW ◯
CORVUS BRACHYRHYNCHOS

DATE_____

LOCATION_____

NOTES_____

_____

FISH CROW ◯
CORVUS OSSIFRAGUS

DATE_____

LOCATION_____

NOTES_____

_____

NORTHWESTERN CROW ◯
CORVUS CAURINUS

DATE_____

LOCATION_____

NOTES_____

_____

TAMAULIPAS CROW (R) ◯
CORVUS IMPARATUS

DATE_____

LOCATION_____

NOTES_____

_____

COMMON RAVEN ◯
CORVUS CORAX

DATE_____

LOCATION_____

NOTES_____

_____

CHIHUAHUAN RAVEN ◯
CORVUS CRYPTOLEUCUS

DATE_____

LOCATION_____

NOTES_____

_____

PARIDAE
(C H I C K A D E E S & T I T M I C E)

BLACK-CAPPED CHICKADEE ◯
POECILE ATRICAPILLA

DATE_____

LOCATION_____

NOTES_____

_____

CAROLINA CHICKADEE ◯
POECILE CAROLINENSIS

DATE_____

LOCATION_____

NOTES_____

_____

MOUNTAIN CHICKADEE ○
POECILE GAMBELI

DATE_____

LOCATION_____

NOTES_____

_____

CHESTNUT-BACKED CHICKADEE ○
POECILE RUFESCENS

DATE_____

LOCATION_____

NOTES_____

_____

MEXICAN CHICKADEE ○
POECILE SCLATEREI

DATE_____

LOCATION_____

NOTES_____

_____

BOREAL CHICKADEE ○
POECILE HUDSONICA

DATE_____

LOCATION_____

NOTES_____

_____

GRAY-HEADED CHICKADEE ○
POECILE CINCTA

DATE_____

LOCATION_____

NOTES_____

_____

TUFTED TITMOUSE ○
BAEOLOPHUS BICOLOR

DATE_____

LOCATION_____

NOTES_____

_____

BLACK-CRESTED TITMOUSE ○
BAEOLOPHUS BICOLOR

DATE_____

LOCATION_____

NOTES_____

_____

OAK TITMOUSE ○
BAEOLOPHUS INORNATUS

DATE_____

LOCATION_____

NOTES_____

_____

JUNIPER TITMOUSE ○
BAEOLOPHUS GRISEUS

DATE_____

LOCATION_____

NOTES_____

_____

BRINDLED TITMOUSE ○
BAEOLOPHUS WOLLWEBERI

DATE_____

LOCATION_____

NOTES_____

_____

SITTIDAE
(NUTHATCHES)

WHITE-BREASTED NUTHATCH ○
SITTA CAROLINENSIS

DATE_____

LOCATION_____

NOTES_____

_____

RED-BREASTED NUTHATCH ○
SITTA CANADENSIS

DATE_____

LOCATION_____

NOTES_____

PYGMY NUTHATCH ○
SITTA PYGMAEA

DATE_____

LOCATION_____

NOTES_____

BROWN-HEADED NUTHATCH ○
SITTA PUSILLA

DATE_____

LOCATION_____

NOTES_____

CERTHIDAE

BROWN CREEPER ○
CERTHIA AMERICANA

DATE_____

LOCATION_____

NOTES_____

TROGLODTIDAE
(WRENS)

HOUSE WREN ○
TROGLODYTES AEDON

DATE_____

LOCATION_____

NOTES_____

WINTER WREN ○
TROGLODYTES TROGLODYTES

DATE_____

LOCATION_____

NOTES_____

BEWICK'S WREN ○
THRYOMANES BEWICKII

DATE_____

LOCATION_____

NOTES_____

CAROLINA WREN ○
THRYOTHORUS LUDOVICIANUS

DATE_____

LOCATION_____

NOTES_____

MARSH WREN ○
CISTOTHORUS PALUSTRIS

DATE_____

LOCATION_____

NOTES_____

SEDGE WREN ○
CISTOTHORUS PLATENSIS

DATE_____

LOCATION_____

NOTES_____

ROCK WREN ○
SALPINCTES OBSOLETUS

DATE_____

LOCATION_____

NOTES_____

CANYON WREN ○
CATHERPES MEXICANUS

DATE_____

LOCATION_____

NOTES_____

_____

CACTUS WREN ○
CAMPYLORHYNCHUS BRUNNEICAPILLUS

DATE_____

LOCATION_____

NOTES_____

_____

WRENTIT ○
CHAMAEA FASCIATA

DATE_____

LOCATION_____

NOTES_____

_____

SYLVIIDAE
(GNATCATCHERS)

BLUE-GRAY GNATCATCHER ○
POLIOPTILA CAERULEA

DATE_____

LOCATION_____

NOTES_____

_____

CALIFORNIA GNATCATCHER ○
POLIOPTILA CALIFORNICA

DATE_____

LOCATION_____

NOTES_____

_____

BLACK-TAILED GNATCATCHER ○
POLIOPTILA MELANURA

DATE_____

LOCATION_____

NOTES_____

_____

BLACK-CAPPED GNATCATCHER (R) ○
POLIOPTILA NIGRICEPS

DATE_____

LOCATION_____

NOTES_____

_____

AEGITHLIDAE

BUSHTIT ○
SALTRIPARUS MINIMUSP

DATE_____

LOCATION_____

NOTES_____

_____

REMZIDAE

VERDIN ○
AURIPARUS FLAVICEPS

DATE_____

LOCATION_____

NOTES_____

_____

REGULIDAE

RUBY-CROWNED KINGLET ○
REGULUS CALENDULA

DATE_____

LOCATION_____

NOTES_____

_____

GOLDEN-CROWNED KINGLET ○
REGULUS SATRAPA

DATE_____

LOCATION_____

NOTES_____

_____

VIRONIDAE
(VIREOS)

YELLOW-THROATED VIREO ○
VIREO FLAVIFRONS

DATE_____

LOCATION_____

NOTES_____

_____

WHITE-EYED VIREO ○
VIREO GRISEUS

DATE_____

LOCATION_____

NOTES_____

_____

HUTTON'S VIREO ○
VIREO HUTTONI

DATE_____

LOCATION_____

NOTES_____

_____

BLACK-CAPPED VIREO ○
VIREO ATRICAPILLUS

DATE_____

LOCATION_____

NOTES_____

_____

BLUE-HEADED VIREO ○
VIREO SOLITARIUS

DATE_____

LOCATION_____

NOTES_____

_____

CASSIN'S VIREO ○
VIREO CASSINII

DATE_____

LOCATION_____

NOTES_____

_____

PLUMBEOUS VIREO ○
VIREO PLUMBEUS

DATE_____

LOCATION_____

NOTES_____

_____

GRAY VIREO ○
VIREO VICINOIR

DATE_____

LOCATION_____

NOTES_____

_____

BELL'S VIREO ○
VIREO BELLII

DATE_____

LOCATION_____

NOTES_____

_____

WARBLING VIREO ○
VIREO GILVUS

DATE_____

LOCATION_____

NOTES_____

_____

RED-EYED VIREO ○
VIREO OLIVACEUS

DATE_____

LOCATION_____

NOTES_____

PHILADELPHIA VIREO ○
VIREO PHILADELPHICUS

DATE_____

LOCATION_____

NOTES_____

BLACK-WHISKERED VIREO ○
VIREO ALTILOQUUS

DATE_____

LOCATION_____

NOTES_____

YELLOW-GREEN VIREO (R) ○
VIREO FLAVOVIRIDIS

DATE_____

LOCATION_____

NOTES_____

PARULIDAE
(W A R B L E R S)

YELLOW WARBLER ○
DENDROICA PETECHIA

DATE_____

LOCATION_____

NOTES_____

CERULEAN WARBLER ○
DENDROICA CERULEA

DATE_____

LOCATION_____

NOTES_____

**BLACK-THROATED
BLUE WARBLER** ○
DENDROICA CAERULESCENS

DATE_____

LOCATION_____

NOTES_____

MYRTLE WARBLER ○
DENDROICA CORONATA

DATE_____

LOCATION_____

NOTES_____

AUDUBON'S WARBLER ○
DENDROICA CORONATA

DATE_____

LOCATION_____

NOTES_____

CAPE MAY WARBLER ○
DENDROICA TIGRINA

DATE_____

LOCATION_____

NOTES_____

MAGNOLIA WARBLER ○
DENDROICA MAGNOLIA

DATE_____

LOCATION_____

NOTES_____

BLACKPOLL WARBLER ○
DENDROICA STRIATA

DATE_____

LOCATION_____

NOTES_____

BAY-BREASTED WARBLER ○
DENDROICA CASTANEA

DATE_____

LOCATION_____

NOTES_____

PINE WARBLER ○
DENDROICA PINUS

DATE_____

LOCATION_____

NOTES_____

BLACK-THROATED GRAY WARBLER ○
DENDROICA NIGRESCENS

DATE_____

LOCATION_____

NOTES_____

BLACK-THROATED GREEN WARBLER ○
DENDROICA VIRENS

DATE_____

LOCATION_____

NOTES_____

TOWNSEND'S WARBLER ○
DENDROICA TOWNSENDI

DATE_____

LOCATION_____

NOTES_____

GOLDEN-CHEEKED WARBLER ○
DENDROICA CHRYSOPARIA

DATE_____

LOCATION_____

NOTES_____

CHESTNUT-SIDED WARBLER ○
DENDROICA PENSYLVANICA

DATE_____

LOCATION_____

NOTES_____

BLACKBURNIAN WARBLER ○
DENDROICA FUSCA

DATE_____

LOCATION_____

NOTES_____

YELLOW-THROATED WARBLER ○
DENDROICA DOMINICA

DATE_____

LOCATION_____

NOTES_____

GRACE'S WARBLER ○
DENDROICA GRACIAE

DATE_____

LOCATION_____

NOTES_____

PALM WARBLER ○
DENDROICA PALMARUM

DATE_____

LOCATION_____

NOTES_____

PRAIRIE WARBLER ○
DENDROICA DISCOLOR

DATE_____

LOCATION_____

NOTES_____

KIRTLAND'S WARBLER ○
DENDROICA KIRTLANDII

DATE_____

LOCATION_____

NOTES_____

YELLOW-BREASTED CHAT ○
ICTERIA VIRENS

DATE_____

LOCATION_____

NOTES_____

PROTHONOTARY WARBLER ○
PROTONOTARIA CITREA

DATE_____

LOCATION_____

NOTES_____

WILSON'S WARBLER ○
WILSONIA PUSILLA

DATE_____

LOCATION_____

NOTES_____

HOODED WARBLER ○
WILSONIA CITRINA

DATE_____

LOCATION_____

NOTES_____

CANADA WARBLER ○
WILSONIA CANADENSIS

DATE_____

LOCATION_____

NOTES_____

NORTHERN PARULA ○
PARULA AMERICANA

DATE_____

LOCATION_____

NOTES_____

TROPICAL PARULA (R) ○
PARULA PITIAYUMI

DATE_____

LOCATION_____

NOTES_____

TENNESSEE WARBLER ○
VERMIVORA PEREGRINA

DATE_____

LOCATION_____

NOTES_____

ORANGE-CROWNED WARBLER ○
VERMIVORA CELATA

DATE_____

LOCATION_____

NOTES_____

BLUE-WINGED WARBLER ○
VERMIVORA PINUS

DATE_____

LOCATION_____

NOTES_____

GOLDEN-WINGED WARBLER ○
VERMIVORA CHRYSOPTERA

DATE_____

LOCATION_____

NOTES_____

BREWSTER'S WARBLER ○
VERMIVORA PINUS X CHRYSOPTERA

DATE_____

LOCATION_____

NOTES_____

_____

LAWRENCE'S WARBLER ○
VERMIVORA PINUS X CHRYSOPTERA

DATE_____

LOCATION_____

NOTES_____

_____

NASHVILLE WARBLER ○
VERMIVORA RUFICAPILLA

DATE_____

LOCATION_____

NOTES_____

_____

VIRGINIA'S WARBLER ○
VERMIVORA VIRGINIAE

DATE_____

LOCATION_____

NOTES_____

_____

COLIMA WARBLER (R) ○
VERMIVORA CRISSALIS

DATE_____

LOCATION_____

NOTES_____

_____

LUCY'S WARBLER ○
VERMIVORA LUCIAE

DATE_____

LOCATION_____

NOTES_____

_____

ARCTIC WARBLER ○
PHYLLOSCOPUS BOREALIS

DATE_____

LOCATION_____

NOTES_____

_____

BLACK AND WHITE WARBLER ○
MNIOTILTA VARIA

DATE_____

LOCATION_____

NOTES_____

_____

OVENBIRD ○
SEIURUS AUROCAPILLUS

DATE_____

LOCATION_____

NOTES_____

_____

NORTHERN WATERTHRUSH ○
SEIURUS NOVEBORACENSIS

DATE_____

LOCATION_____

NOTES_____

_____

LOUISIANA WATERTHRUSH ○
SEIRUS MOTACILLA

DATE_____

LOCATION_____

NOTES_____

_____

WORM-EATING WARBLER ○
HELMITHEROS VERMIVORUS

DATE_____

LOCATION_____

NOTES_____

_____

SWAINSON'S WARBLER ○
LIMNOTHLYPIS SWAINSONII

DATE_____

LOCATION_____

NOTES_____

_____

COMMON YELLOWTHROAT ○
GEOTHLYPIS TRICHAS

DATE_____

LOCATION_____

NOTES_____

_____

KENTUCKY WARBLER ○
OPORORNIS FORMOSUS

DATE_____

LOCATION_____

NOTES_____

_____

MACGILLIVRAY'S WARBLER ○
OPORORNIS TOLMIEI

DATE_____

LOCATION_____

NOTES_____

_____

MOURNING WARBLER ○
OPORORNIS PHILADELPHIA

DATE_____

LOCATION_____

NOTES_____

_____

CONNECTICUT WARBLER ○
OPORORNIS AGILIS

DATE_____

LOCATION_____

NOTES_____

_____

AMERICAN REDSTART ○
SETOPHAGA RUTICILLA

DATE_____

LOCATION_____

NOTES_____

_____

RED-FACED WARBLER ○
CARDELLINA RUBRIFRONS

DATE_____

LOCATION_____

NOTES_____

_____

PAINTED REDSTART ○
MYIBORUS PICTUS

DATE_____

LOCATION_____

NOTES_____

_____

OLIVE WARBLER ○
PEUCEDRAMUS TAENIATUS

DATE_____

LOCATION_____

NOTES_____

_____

RUFOUS-CAPPED WARBLER (R) ○
BASILEUTERUS RUFIFRONS

DATE_____

LOCATION_____

NOTES_____

_____

BANAQUIT (R) ○
COEREBA FLAVEOLA

DATE_____

LOCATION_____

NOTES_____

_____

THRAUPIDAE
(TANAGERS)

SUMMER TANAGER ○
PIRANGA RUBRA

DATE_____

LOCATION_____

NOTES_____

_____

SCARLET TANAGER ○
PIRANGA OLIVACEA

DATE_____

LOCATION_____

NOTES_____

_____

WESTERN TANAGER ○
PIRANGA LUDOVICIANA

DATE_____

LOCATION_____

NOTES_____

_____

HEPATIC TANAGER ○
PIRANGA FLAVA

DATE_____

LOCATION_____

NOTES_____

_____

FLAME-COLORED TANAGER (R) ○
PIRANGA BIDENTATA

DATE_____

LOCATION_____

NOTES_____

_____

WESTERN SPINDALIS (R) ○
SPENDALIS ZENA

DATE_____

LOCATION_____

NOTES_____

_____

STURNIDAE

EUROPEAN STARLING (I) ○
STURNUS VULGARIS

DATE_____

LOCATION_____

NOTES_____

_____

CRESTED MYNA (I) ○
ACRIDOTHERES CRISTATELLUS

DATE_____

LOCATION_____

NOTES_____

_____

COMMON MYNA (I) ○
ACRIDOTHERES TRISTIS

DATE_____

LOCATION_____

NOTES_____

_____

HILL MYNA (I) ○
GRACULA RELIGIOSA

DATE_____

LOCATION_____

NOTES_____

_____

ICTERIDAE
(BLACKBIRDS)

YELLOW-HEADED BLACKBIRD ○
XANTHOCEPHALUS XANTHOCEPHALUS

DATE_____

LOCATION_____

NOTES_____

_____

WESTERN MEADOWLARK ○
STURNELLA NEGLECTA

DATE_____

LOCATION_____

NOTES_____

_____

EASTERN MEADOWLARK ○
STURNELLA MAGNA

DATE_____

LOCATION_____

NOTES_____

_____

BOBOLINK ○
DOLICHONYX ORYZOVORUS

DATE_____

LOCATION_____

NOTES_____

_____

COMMON GRACKLE ○
QUISCALUS QUISCULA

DATE_____

LOCATION_____

NOTES_____

_____

BOAT-TAILED GRACKLE ○
QUISCALUS MAJOR

DATE_____

LOCATION_____

NOTES_____

_____

GREAT-TAILED GRACKLE ○
QUISCULUS MEXICANUS

DATE_____

LOCATION_____

NOTES_____

_____

RED-WINGED BLACKBIRD ○
AGELAIUS PHOENICEUS

DATE_____

LOCATION_____

NOTES_____

_____

TRI-COLORED BLACKBIRD ○
AGELAIUS TRICOLOR

DATE_____

LOCATION_____

NOTES_____

_____

BROWN-HEADED COWBIRD ○
MOLOTHRUS ATER

DATE_____

LOCATION_____

NOTES_____

_____

BRONZED COWBIRD ○
MOLOTHRUS AENEUS

DATE_____

LOCATION_____

NOTES_____

_____

SHINY COWBIRD (R) ○
MOLOTHRUS BONARIENSIS

DATE_____

LOCATION_____

NOTES_____

_____

BREWER'S BLACKBIRD ○
EUPHAGUS CYANOCEPHALUS

DATE_____

LOCATION_____

NOTES_____

_____

RUSTY BLACKBIRD ○
EUPHAGUS CAROLINUS

DATE_____

LOCATION_____

NOTES_____

_____

BALTIMORE ORIOLE ○
ICTERUS GALBULA

DATE_____

LOCATION_____

NOTES_____

_____

BULLOCK'S ORIOLE ○
ICTERUS BULLOCKII

DATE_____

LOCATION_____

NOTES_____

_____

HOODED ORIOLE ○
ICTERUS CUCULLATUS

DATE_____

LOCATION_____

NOTES_____

_____

ORCHARD ORIOLE ○
ICTERUS SPURIUS

DATE_____

LOCATION_____

NOTES_____

_____

SCOTT'S ORIOLE ○
ICTERUS PARISORUM

DATE_____

LOCATION_____

NOTES_____

_____

ALTAMIRA ORIOLE ○
ICTERUS GULARIS

DATE_____

LOCATION_____

NOTES_____

_____

AUDUBON'S ORIOLE ○
ICTERUS GRADUACAUDA

DATE_____

LOCATION_____

NOTES_____

_____

SPOT-BREASTED ORIOLE ○
ICTURUS PECTORALIS

DATE_____

LOCATION_____

NOTES_____

_____

STREAK-BACKED ORIOLE (R) ○
ICTERUS PUTULATUS

DATE_____

LOCATION_____

NOTES_____

_____

PASSERIDAE
(OLD WORLD SPARROWS)

HOUSE SPARROW (I) ○
PASSER DOMISTICUS

DATE_____

LOCATION_____

NOTES_____

_____

EURASIAN TREE SPARROW (I) ○
PASSER MONTANUS

DATE_____

LOCATION_____

NOTES_____

_____

EMBERZIDAE
(SPARROWS)

DICKCISSEL ○
SPIZA AMERICANA

DATE_____

LOCATION_____

NOTES_____

_____

LARK BUNTING ○
CALAMOSPIZA MELANOCORYS

DATE_____

LOCATION_____

NOTES_____

_____

SONG SPARROW ○
MELOSPIZA MELODIA

DATE_____

LOCATION_____

NOTES_____

_____

LINCOLN'S SPARROW ○
MELOSPIZA LINCOLNII

DATE_____

LOCATION_____

NOTES_____

_____

SWAMP SPARROW ○
MELOSPIZA GEORGIANA

DATE_____

LOCATION_____

NOTES_____

_____

FOX SPARROW ○
PASSERELLA ILIACA

DATE_____

LOCATION_____

NOTES_____

_____

RUFOUS-CROWNED SPARROW ○
AIMOPHILA RUFICEPS

DATE_____

LOCATION_____

NOTES_____

_____

CASSIN'S SPARROW ○
AIMOPHILA CASSINII

DATE_____

LOCATION_____

NOTES_____

_____

BOTTERI'S SPARROW ○
AIMOPHILA BOTTERII

DATE_____

LOCATION_____

NOTES_____

_____

BACHMAN'S SPARROW ○
AIMOPHILA AESTIVALIS

DATE_____

LOCATION_____

NOTES_____

_____

RUFOUS-WINGED SPARROW ○
AIMOPHILA CARPALIS

DATE_____

LOCATION_____

NOTES_____

_____

FIVE-STRIPED SPARROW (R) ○
AIMOPHILA QUINQUESTRIATA

DATE_____

LOCATION_____

NOTES_____

_____

CHIPPING SPARROW ○
SPIZELLA PASSERINA

DATE_____

LOCATION_____

NOTES_____

_____

FIELD SPARROW ○
SPIZELLA PUSILLA

DATE_____

LOCATION_____

NOTES_____

_____

CLAY-COLORED SPARROW ○
SPIZELLA PALLIDA

DATE_____

LOCATION_____

NOTES_____

_____

BREWER'S SPARROW ○
SPIZELLA BREWERI

DATE_____

LOCATION_____

NOTES_____

_____

TREE SPARROW ○
SPIZELLA ARBOREA

DATE_____

LOCATION_____

NOTES_____

_____

BLACK-CHINNED SPARROW ○
SPIZELLA ATROGULARIS

DATE_____

LOCATION_____

NOTES_____

_____

LARK SPARROW ○
CHONDESTES GRAMMACUS

DATE_____

LOCATION_____

NOTES_____

_____

BLACK-THROATED SPARROW ○
AMPHISPIZA BILINEATA

DATE_____

LOCATION_____

NOTES_____

_____

SAGE SPARROW ○
AMPHISPIZA BELLI

DATE_____

LOCATION_____

NOTES_____

_____

SAVANNAH SPARROW ○
PASSERCULUS SANDWICHENSIS

DATE_____

LOCATION_____

NOTES_____

_____

VESPER SPARROW ○
POOECESTES GRAMINEUS

DATE_____

LOCATION_____

NOTES_____

_____

HENSLOW'S SPARROW ○
AMMODRAMUS HENSLOWII

DATE_____

LOCATION_____

NOTES_____

_____

BAIRD'S SPARROW ○
AMMODRAMUS BAIRDII

DATE_____

LOCATION_____

NOTES_____

_____

GRASSHOPPER SPARROW ○
AMMODRAMUS SAVANNARUM

DATE_____

LOCATION_____

NOTES_____

_____

LE CONTE'S SPARROW ○
AMMODRAMUS LECONTEII

DATE_____

LOCATION_____

NOTES_____

SALTMARSH SHARP-TAILED SPARROW ○
AMMODRAMUS CAUDACUTUS

DATE_____

LOCATION_____

NOTES_____

_____

NELSON'S SHARP-TAILED SPARROW ○
AMMODRAMUS NELSONI

DATE_____

LOCATION_____

NOTES_____

_____

SEASIDE SPARROW ○
AMMODRAMUS MARITIMUS

DATE_____

LOCATION_____

NOTES_____

_____

WHITE-THROATED SPARROW ○
ZONOTRICHIA ALBICOLLIS

DATE_____

LOCATION_____

NOTES_____

_____

WHITE-CROWNED SPARROW ○
ZONOTRICHIA LEUCOPHRYS

DATE_____

LOCATION_____

NOTES_____

_____

GOLDEN-CROWNED SPARROW ○
ZONOTRICHIA ATRICAPILLA

DATE_____

LOCATION_____

NOTES_____

_____

HARRIS'S SPARROW ○
ZONOTRICHIA QUERULA

DATE_____

LOCATION_____

NOTES_____

_____

SLATE-COLORED JUNCO ○
JUNCO HYEMALIS

DATE_____

LOCATION_____

NOTES_____

_____

OREGON JUNCO ○
JUNCO HYEMALIS

DATE_____

LOCATION_____

NOTES_____

_____

PINK-SIDED JUNCO ○
JUNCO HYEMALIS

DATE_____

LOCATION_____

NOTES_____

_____

WHITE-WINGED JUNCO ○
JUNCO HYEMALIS

DATE_____

LOCATION_____

NOTES_____

_____

GRAY-HEADED JUNCO ○
JUNCO HYEMALIS

DATE_____

LOCATION_____

NOTES_____

_____

RED-BACKED JUNCO ○
JUNCO HYEMALIS

DATE_____

LOCATION_____

NOTES_____

_____

LAPLAND LONGSPUR ○
CALCARIUS LAPPONICUS

DATE_____

LOCATION_____

NOTES_____

_____

SMITH'S LONGSPUR ○
CALCARIUS PICTUS

DATE_____

LOCATION_____

NOTES_____

_____

CHESTNUT-COLLARED LONGSPUR ○
CALCARIUS ORNATUS

DATE_____

LOCATION_____

NOTES_____

_____

MCCOWN'S LONGSPUR ○
CALCARIUS MCCOWNII

DATE_____

LOCATION_____

NOTES_____

_____

SNOW BUNTING ○
PLECTROPHENAX NIVALIS

DATE_____

LOCATION_____

NOTES_____

_____

MCKAY'S BUNTING ○
PLECTROPHENAX HYPERBOREUS

DATE_____

LOCATION_____

NOTES_____

_____

RUFOUS-SIDED TOWHEE ○
PIPILO ERYTHROPHTHALMUS

DATE_____

LOCATION_____

NOTES_____

_____

SPOTTED TOWHEE ○
PIPILO MACULATUS

DATE_____

LOCATION_____

NOTES_____

_____

CALIFORNIA TOWHEE ○
PIPILO CRISSALIS

DATE_____

LOCATION_____

NOTES_____

_____

CANYON TOWHEE ○
PIPILO FUSCUS

DATE_____

LOCATION_____

NOTES_____

_____

ABERT'S TOWHEE ○
PIPILO ABERTI

DATE_____

LOCATION_____

NOTES_____

_____

WHITE-COLLARED SEEDEATER (R) ○
SPOROPHILA TORQUEOLA

DATE_____

LOCATION_____

NOTES_____

_____

GREEN-TAILED TOWHEE ○
PIPILO CHLORURUS

DATE_____

LOCATION_____

NOTES_____

_____

OLIVE SPARROW (R) ○
ARREMONOPS RUFIVIRGATUS

DATE_____

LOCATION_____

NOTES_____

_____

FRINGILLIDAE
(FINCHES)

BROWN-CAPPED ROSY FINCH ○
LEUCOSTICTE AUSTRALIS

DATE_____

LOCATION_____

NOTES_____

_____

BLACK-CAPPED ROSY FINCH ○
LEUCOSTICTE ATRATA

DATE_____

LOCATION_____

NOTES_____

_____

GRAY-CAPPED ROSY FINCH ○
LEUCOSTICTE TEPHROCOTIS

DATE_____

LOCATION_____

NOTES_____

_____

HOUSE FINCH ○
CARPODACUS MEXICANUS

DATE_____

LOCATION_____

NOTES_____

_____

PURPLE FINCH ○
CARPODACUS PURPUREUS

DATE_____

LOCATION_____

NOTES_____

_____

CASSIN'S FINCH ○
CARPODACUS CASSINII

DATE_____

LOCATION_____

NOTES_____

_____

RED CROSSBILL ○
LOXIA CURVIROSTRA

DATE_____

LOCATION_____

NOTES_____

_____

WHITE-WINGED CROSSBILL ○
LOXIA LEUCOPTERA

DATE_____

LOCATION_____

NOTES_____

_____

PINE GROSBEAK ○
PINICOLA ENUCLEATOR

DATE_____

LOCATION_____

NOTES_____

_____

BRAMBLING ○
FRINGILLA MONTIFRINGILLA

DATE_____

LOCATION_____

NOTES_____

_____

COMMON REDPOLL ○
CARDUELIS FLAMMEA

DATE_____

LOCATION_____

NOTES_____

_____

HOARY REDPOLL ○
CARDUELIS HORNEMANNI

DATE_____

LOCATION_____

NOTES_____

_____

GOLDFINCH ○
CARDUELIS TRISTIS

DATE_____

LOCATION_____

NOTES_____

_____

PINE SISKIN ○
CARDUELIS PINUS

DATE_____

LOCATION_____

NOTES_____

_____

LESSER GOLDFINCH ◯
CARDUELIS PSALTRIA

DATE_____

LOCATION_____

NOTES_____

LAWRENCE'S GOLDFINCH ◯
CARDUELIS LAWRENCEI

DATE_____

LOCATION_____

NOTES_____

EUROPEAN GOLDFINCH (I) ◯
CARDUELIS CARDUELIS

DATE_____

LOCATION_____

NOTES_____

EVENING GROSBEAK ◯
COCCOTHRAUSTES VESPERTINUS

DATE_____

LOCATION_____

NOTES_____

CARDINALIDAE
(GROSBEAKS)

NORTHERN CARDINAL ◯
CARDINALIS CARDINALIS

DATE_____

LOCATION_____

NOTES_____

PYRRHULOXIA ◯
CARDINALIS SINUATUS

DATE_____

LOCATION_____

NOTES_____

BLUE GROSBEAK ◯
GUIRACA CAERULEA

DATE_____

LOCATION_____

NOTES_____

INDIGO BUNTING ◯
PASSERINA CYANEA

DATE_____

LOCATION_____

NOTES_____

LAZULI BUNTING ◯
PASSERINA AMOENA

DATE_____

LOCATION_____

NOTES_____

PAINTED BUNTING ◯
PASSERINA CIRIS

DATE_____

LOCATION_____

NOTES_____

VARIED BUNTING ◯
PASSERINA VERSICOLOR

DATE_____

LOCATION_____

NOTES_____

BLUE BUNTING (R) ◯
CYANOCOMPSA PARELLINA

DATE_____

LOCATION_____

NOTES_____

ROSE-BREASTED GROSBEAK ○
PHEUCTICUS LUDOVICIANUS

DATE_____

LOCATION_____

NOTES_____

_____

BLACK-HEADED GROSBEAK ○
PHEUCTICUS MELANOCEPHALUS

DATE_____

LOCATION_____

NOTES_____

_____

INDEX

INDEX

INDEX

INDEX

INDEX

INDEX

INDEX

INDEX

INDEX

INDEX

INDEX

Naturalist Scott Shupe's thirty-year career interpreting nature and wildlife for the lay public has included working with state and federal agencies as well as private zoos and wildlife attractions. He has worked as a wild-life cameraman, served as host and narrator for nature-oriented television programming and has appeared as a guest naturalist in nature and outdoor television programs airing on PBS and The Outdoor Channel. He is also the founder and original owner of the Natural History Educational Company, an organiza-tion of professional naturalists providing con-servation education programming to schools throughout the southeastern United States.

As an accomplished wildlife photogra-pher and author, his photographs and nature writings have appeared in dozens of nature-oriented publications. From 1991 through 2001, he was the director and co-owner of a private nature center in Ken-tucky. In 1996 he was awarded the Jesse Stuart Media award for the production of a series of instructional life science video programs marketed to schools and libraries nationwide. He has been named Naturalist of the Year by the Kentucky Society of Naturalists and awarded the Environmental Stewardship Award by the Kentucky Environmental Quality Commission. Like many naturalists, he consid-ers himself to be a "jack-of-all-trades and master of none" when it comes the study of wildlife. A devoted and life-long birder who has worked professionally with birds of prey, he has twice received recognition from the U.S. Fish & Wildlife Service for his contribution to the conservation of America's raptors. He has held U.S. Fish & Wildlife Service Permits for Threatened and Endangered Species, fed-eral Special Purpose Permits for the possession of protected raptors, USDA-Aphis Permits for possession of wild mammal species, and has been variously licensed and permitted for the possession of protected species for educational purposes by state wildlife agencies in 30 states.

He is also a recognized expert in the field of herpetology and is the author of *U.S. Guide to Venomous Snakes and their Mimics* by Stoeger Publishing. He began his professional career working as a herpetologist in Florida where he was employed at two major reptile attractions and a venom laboratory. Today he is still active in the study of America's reptiles and amphibians, currently serving as Director of Education for the Kentucky Reptile Zoo & Venom Laboratory located in Slade, Kentucky.

He has traveled extensively throughout the North American continent, from Alaska to Belize, observing, photographing and filming wildlife. He and his wife Lisa make their home in rural western Kentucky on a ninety-acre farm now man-aged as a private wildlife refuge.